THE TREE OF LIFE

THE TREE OF LIFE

Image for the Cosmos

ROGER COOK

With 165 illustrations, 31 in color

THAMES AND HUDSON

© 1974 Roger Cook
Reprinted 1992

Published in the United States in 1988 by
Thames and Hudson Inc., 500 Fifth Avenue,
New York, New York 10110

Library of Congress Catalog Card Number
88-50248

Printed and bound in Yugoslavia

Contents

ACKNOWLEDGMENTS

Objects in the plates are reproduced by courtesy of the following:
Accademia, Florence 49
American Museum of Natural History, New York 60
Ashmolean Museum, Oxford 29
Bayerische Staatsbibliothek, Munich 44
Bibliotheek der Rijksuniversiteit, Leiden 39 (Cod. Voss. 29)
Bibliothèque Nationale, Paris 25 (MS. suppl. turc 190); 52 (MS. hébreu 7)
Bodleian Library, Oxford 33 (MS. Ouseley add. 176)
Collection of Dr Edwin Binney, 3rd 20
British Museum, London 2, 3, 4, 21, 31, 34, 43, 53 (MS. Nero C. IV)
Cathedral treasury, Gerona 41
Galleria Schwarz, Milan 56
Indian Museum, Calcutta 7
Metropolitan Museum of Art, New York, Gift of J. Pierpont Morgan, 1911 12
Munson-Williams-Proctor Institute, New York 65
Musée Guimet, Paris 13, 18
Musée National d'Art Moderne, Paris 57
Museo Arqueólogico Nacional, Madrid 54
Museum für Völkerkunde, Berlin 55
Museum of Navaho Ceremonial Life, Santa Fe, N.Mex. 5
Nelson Gallery – Atkins Museum, Kansas City, Mo. (Nelson Fund) 19
Pasadena Museum of Modern Art, Galka E. Schreyer Blue Four Collection 58 (53.25)
Philadelphia Museum of Art, the A.E. Gallatin Collection 62 (J52-61-82)
Public Museums, Liverpool 6
Sächsische Landesbibliothek, Dresden 42
Smithsonian Institution, Freer Gallery of Art, Washington D.C. 24
Trinity College Library, Cambridge 40 (MS. R. 16.2)
Universitätsbibliothek, Würzburg 48 (M.p.th.)
Universitetsbibliotheket, Uppsala 32
University of Missouri Library 9
Victoria and Albert Museum, London 14, 17, 22, 23, 45, 63

Photographs supplied by the following:
Alinari 46, 47, figs. 22, 76
Anderson fig. 20
Antikvarisk Topografiska Arkivet, Stockholm (H. Faith-Ell) 51
Father B. Bagatti fig. 73
Belseaux/Zodiaque figs. 54, 74
Collection Janet Bord fig. 3
Caisse Nationale des Monuments Historiques 36
Peter Clayton fig. 32
Daily Telegraph Colour Library 61
Department of Archaeology, Government of India 7
M. Dragu 93
Walter Dräyer fig. 59
Edinburgh University Library fig. 47
Giraudon figs. 19, 53
André Held 9, 11, fig. 57
Hirmer Fotoarchiv Munich 2, 4
Martin Hürlimann 27, 35, fig. 55
Jacqueline Hyde 13, 17, 57
India Office Library fig. 58
Mircea Iuga fig. 95
Japan Information Centre, London 8
Jeifer fig. 24
Victor Kennett fig. 5
Richard Lannoy 15, 64, figs. 27, 28
E. J. Lindgren fig. 96
Mansell-Alinari fig. 68
Mas 41, 54
Wayne Miller, Ovinda, Calif. 91
Popperfoto fig. 4
Josephine Powell 16
Boris de Rachewiltz fig. 38
Radio Times Hulton Picture Library fig. 37
N. Sandelescu fig. 94
Scala 49
Staatliches Museum für Völkerkunde, Munich fig. 58
Eileen Tweedy 1, 14, 18, 21, 22, fig. 31
Universitets Oldsaksamling, Oslo 50
Victoria and Albert Museum, London fig. 6
P.S. Voigt fig. 75

The Tree of Imagination

'The Nature of Visionary Fancy or Imagination, is very little known, & the Eternal nature & permanence of its ever Existent Images is considered as less permanent than the things of Vegetative and Generative Nature; yet the Oak dies as well as the Lettuce, but its Eternal Image & Individuality never dies but returns by its seed; just so the Imaginative Image returns by the seed of Contemplative Thought.'

Since 1810, when William Blake wrote these words, the whole of mankind's imaginative life, as expressed in myth and symbol, has opened out before us. Thanks to the rapid advance in communication provided by modern technology, a glance through the pictures in this book is enough to confirm the truth of Blake's statement that 'the Imaginative Image returns by the seed of Contemplative Thought.' Throughout the world, at all times and in all places, men have pictured, in one form or another, the imaginative image of the tree.

But what exactly does Blake mean by 'imaginative image'? Evidently he is alluding to a special way of seeing, a mode of vision different from the one by which we normally 'see' the world. A statement by a modern American Indian, a visionary, whom Blake would have hailed as a brother, can help us here. He too 'saw' a tree:

'Then I was standing on the highest mountain of them all, and round about beneath me was the whole hoop of the world. And while I stood there I saw more than I can tell and I understood more than I saw; for I was seeing in a sacred manner the shapes of all things in the spirit, and the shape of all shapes as they must live together like one being. And I saw the sacred hoop of my people was one of the many hoops that made one circle, wide as daylight and as starlight, and in the centre grew one mighty flowering tree to shelter all the children of one mother and one father. And I saw that it was holy.'

These words from the autobiography of Black Elk, a holy man of the Oglala Sioux, recall another vision, another time.

'And [the angel] shewed me a pure river of water of life, clear as crystal, proceeding out of the throne of God and of the Lamb. In the midst of the street of it, and on either side of the river, was . . . the tree of life, which bare twelve manner of fruits, and yielded her fruits every month; and the leaves of the tree were for the healing of the nations.'

This is the biblical image of the Tree of Life as it appears in the Revelation of St John (22:1–2). By placing it alongside the vision of Black Elk one realizes that this vision too was 'seen', not simply fabricated or 'imagined' in the pejorative sense. Unfortunately it is in just this sense that we most usually think of imagination. For the scientific bias of our education tends to make us associate the imaginary with the illusory and unreal. This bias has its roots in the eighteenth-century Enlightenment and its cult of reason. Since then the rationalistic bias of modern education has tended to give credence only to the two realms of experience upon which the natural sciences are based: reason and sense perception. In the light of these two, the intermediary realm of imagination gradually faded into the background. No longer recognized as a universally valid mode of perception and cognition, it became, especially during the latter part of the nineteenth century, the exclusive prerogative of a minority of aesthetes and art-lovers.

It was against this that Blake so prophetically protested. He realized that the rising empiricism of the natural sciences would relegate imagination to the vagaries of a 'personalistic' inner world, without proper structure, foundation, or reality. For him, imagination was neither vague, unreal nor 'merely subjective': on the contrary, it described a precise order of reality, pertaining to a definite mode of being with a coherent structure of its own. And Blake was not alone in experiencing it as such. For all the Romantics, poets, painters and philosophers alike, affirmed the structural coherence of imagination, and rebelled against the tyranny of a technical and mechanical reason which threatened the imaginative basis of all human experience.

In order to help re-establish imagination as a faculty with a real cognitive value, Henry Corbin has suggested that the word 'imaginary' might be replaced, when necessary, with the more affirmative word 'imaginal', derived from the Latin word *imaginalis*. Corbin found it necessary to use this word when writing about the visionary experiences of Islamic mystics. For these philosophers recognized a real plane of experience which they called the *'alam al-mithal*, the world of the image, or the *'alam-i-malakut*, the world of imagination. This they conceived as an intermediary realm, existing between, and interpenetrating with, the realms of intellect and sense perception. According to this schema, imagination is the central faculty, that of the soul, acting as a vital bridge between senses and intellect, mind and body, spirit and matter.

This structuring of experience has its roots in the extremely ancient mythological idea of the threefold structure of the cosmos, often expressed in the image of a tree. The Tree of Life, or Cosmic Tree, penetrates the three zones of heaven, earth and underworld, its branches penetrating the celestial world and its roots descending into the abyss. Like the Tree, imagination unites heaven and earth; it is 'rooted' both above and below. Uniting the luminous world of consciousness to the dark underworld of the unconscious, and drawing nourishment from both the 'heavenly-immaterial' world of intelligible meaning and the 'earthly-material' world of sensory perception, it creates the 'magical' intermediary world of images. It is this lively mediation between these opposed worlds that accounts for the multiplicity of symbolism: the fact that a single archetypal image, like the Tree, can produce throughout space and time such an abundant flowering and branching of images.

Like the Tree, imagination is a source of endless regeneration. It is both old and young, and has its autumns and its springs: for if the senses become too heavy and attached to traditional forms, imagination deserts them. It discards old meanings, shatters fixed dogmas, and revives eternal truths, for ever re-clothing them in the light of the new. For, as the French philosopher Gaston Bachelard has observed, 'The imagination is a tree. It has the integrative virtues of a tree. It is root and boughs. It lives between earth and sky. It lives in the earth and in the wind. The imagined tree imperceptibly becomes the cosmological tree, the tree which epitomizes a universe, which makes a universe.'

The Tree at the Centre

The image of the Cosmic Tree or Tree of Life belongs to a coherent body of myths, rites, images and symbols which together make up what the historian of religion Mircea Eliade has called the 'symbolism of the Centre'. Since all symbolic images of the Tree participate, to some degree, in this symbolism, it is important to grasp its basic outlines at the outset. This can be done provisionally with the help of a diagram.

Eliade has shown how all aspects of mankind's 'mythical behaviour' reflect an intense desire to grasp the essential reality of the world. This is particularly evident in man's obsession with the origins of things, with which all myths are ultimately concerned. The centre is, first and foremost, the point of 'absolute beginning' where the latent energies of the sacred first broke through; where the supernatural beings of myth, or the gods or God of religion, first created man and the world. Ultimately all creation takes place at this point, which represents the ultimate source of reality. In the symbolic language of myth and religion it is often referred to as the 'navel of the world', 'Divine Egg', 'Hidden Seed' or 'Root of Roots'; and it is also imagined as a vertical axis, the 'cosmic axis' or 'axis of the world' (Axis Mundi) which stands at the centre of the Universe and passes through the middle of the three cosmic zones, sky, earth and underworld. It is fixed at the heavenly end to either the Pole Star or the sun, the fixed points around which the heavenly bodies rotate. From here it descends through the disc of the earth into the world below.

This idea of the cosmic axis and the 'centre of the world', which is extremely ancient (fourth or third millennium BC) and widely diffused, is embodied primarily in three images, which are to be found in a great variety of forms throughout the world. These are the Pillar or Pole, the Tree and the Mountain. In the diagram all three are represented in features derived from sacred architecture, and in particular from the pyramid-ziggurat (Egypt, Mesopotamia and Mexico) and the Buddhist stupa (India, East Asia). These (pls. 7, 8) represent the Cosmic Mountain or primeval mound (image of both the cosmos and the world), which according to many ancient cosmogonies arose out of the infinite depths of the primordial ocean 'in the beginning'. In the diagram the summit of this Cosmic Mountain is represented as circular, and its base square. These basic geometric forms, and their three-dimensional counterparts, the sphere and the cube, traditionally symbolize Heaven and Earth. On each side, leading to the summit, is a ladder or stairway which serves as a reminder of the many myths, rites and symbols of ascension associated with all symbols of the Axis Mundi. On the summit, at the centre of the radial cross of the four directions, stands the Cosmic Tree, represented by seven discs. These stand for the seven (sometimes it is nine) planetary heavens.

The point where the Axis Mundi pierces the square base of the Mountain is at the centre of a flat spiral. This represents the long and difficult initiatory path which leads towards the centre. The myths, legends and fairytales of the world stress that many difficulties must be overcome (trials of strength, combats with ferocious beasts, etc.) in order to arrive at the centre (achieve the goal, win the maiden, capture the treasure). One can imagine this spiral continuing in the form of a labyrinth beyond the walls of the sanctuary in which the Cosmic Mountain stands.

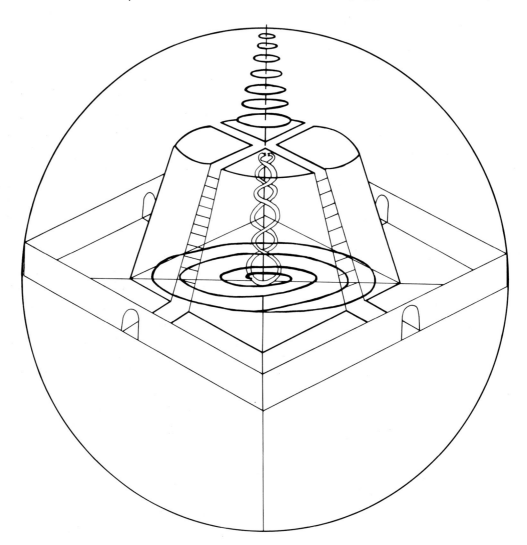

These walls (pl. 31) mark the boundary between the sacred and the profane, and, like the labyrinth, are a means of defence against the demonic forces of chaos which continually threaten the centre. Throughout history there have been many rites of circumambulation to strengthen the magical defences of sacred spaces, city and temple walls. It is on these boundaries that guardian deities appear, as monstrous masks and gargoyles, with the double purpose of frightening the uninitiated and warding off evil spirits. These illustrate what is often called the 'ambivalence of the sacred'. For man both fears and venerates the sacred, experiencing it as the manifestation of an awesome and tremendous power which transcends everything human or cosmic. Yet, paradoxically, this supernatural and transcendent power reveals itself to men through things both human and cosmic. Sky, earth, plant, stone, animal and tree can all appear charged with the supernatural. It is then that these familiar things seem unfamiliar, that they awaken those mixed feelings of adoration and dread that characterize the supra-rational element in religious experience.

From the flat spiral at the base of the Mountain in the diagram rises a double helix made up of intertwined serpents. This, like the stairway, is a symbol of ascent; but this time it is the 'internalized' ascent of ascetic and meditative disciplines such as Kundalini Yoga, where the body itself is conceived as a microcosm. The serpent is very often found in relation to symbols of the centre; for example, the serpent with the tree in the midst of the garden in Genesis, the serpent that is often found coiled around representations of the Cosmic Egg, and the many dragons that guard symbolic equivalents for the centre in mythology and folklore. The serpent's association with the feminine, especially with the Mother Goddess (mistress of the earth, the beasts and fertility), is derived from its earthbound, vital, rhythmically undulating movement; its shape gives it a special association with sexual energy; and its periodic rebirth (through sloughing its skin) associates it with the cyclic changes of the moon. It embodies the regenerative powers of the waters, ruled by the moon, and the latent energies contained within the body of the earth. In the diagram, the traditional ambivalence of the serpent is suggested in its doubled image, for as representative of the vital force it is both creative and destructive. This twofold nature represents the marriage of opposites, and their synthesis into a higher form.

This regenerative double nature of the serpent is one with the ambivalence of the sacred which flows throughout the cosmos, and is the vital sap which passes through the Cosmic Tree. This is the much sought-after 'elixir of immortality', the magic honey-mead, the fire-water of the gods. The Tree, too, incorporates this serpentine and lunar symbolism, for it sheds its bark and leaves and is reborn in the spring, growing rhythmically with the monthly waxing and waning of the moon.

Perhaps the clearest single mythical exposition of the Cosmic Tree is in the Scandinavian Eddas, written down in the tenth to twelfth centuries but clearly very much older. In a dark, foreboding poem, the *Völuspá*, a seeress tells of the fate of the gods and of the end of the world, the Ragnarök. Awoken from a deep sleep, by the great god Odin, she declares:

> *I remember the giants born at the dawn of time,*
> *And those who first gave birth to me.*
> *I know of nine worlds, nine spheres covered by the tree of the world,*
> *That tree set up in wisdom which grows down to the bosom of the earth.*

An Ash I know, Yggdrasil its name,
With water white is the great tree wet;
Thence come its dews that fall in the dales,
Green by Urd's well does it ever grow.

Yggdrasil stands at the centre of three cosmic planes. Its three great roots descend into a tripartite underworld: Hel, the land of the dead; the kingdom of the frost giants; and the underworld realm of the gods, the Aesir, where they assemble every day by the sacred spring of Fate, the Well of Urd, to sit in judgment and settle disputes. The trunk passes through the second plane, Midgard, Middle Earth, the land of mortals; and its branches ascend into Asgard, the heavenly world of the gods. At the base of the tree is the Spring of Mimir (Remembrance), where Odin once sacrificed an eye for a draught of its wisdom.

Three Norns, goddesses of Fate, water the roots of the great tree night and day, while a gigantic serpent, Niogghr, perpetually gnaws at them. These goddesses represent the three faces of the moon goddess: the waxing, fullness and waning of the heavenly body concerned, above all, with the rhythms of life. The three sit at the foot of Yggdrasil, passing the cosmic shuttle between them and weaving the fates of men and the world. They water the roots from the Well of Urd around which they sit, presiding over the 'irrational' world of seeds and latencies, of germinating forms: Water, Chaos and Night.

The serpent is the adversary of the eagle which lives in the topmost branches of the tree. Here also is the seat of Odin, from which he surveys 'the nine worlds covered by the tree'. Various creatures live in, or off, the tree: a squirrel runs up and down its trunk, and horned creatures, harts and goats, devour its branches, leaves and tender shoots. These animals, continually attacking and devouring the tree, coupled with the image of the Norns perpetually watering its roots, form an image of the cyclic processes of time, the endless regeneration of the cosmos – as does the perennial strife between the eagle and the snake, which symbolize the solar and lunar principles (pl. 50).

The theme of rebirth, along with the union of opposites, is present in another image: At Ragnarök, the great tree is said to shake, bringing about the destruction of the gods and the world. However, concealed within its trunk are the seeds of the world's renewal, in the form of a man and woman, from whose union a new race will appear to repopulate the world.

The Tree of Fertility

'Above the wide and motionless deep, under the nine spheres and seven storeys of heaven, at the most central place, the navel of the earth, earth's stillest place, where the moon does not wane and the sun does not set, where eternal summer reigns and the cuckoo calls unceasingly, there the White Youth found himself.'

Thus begins the creation myth of the Yakut tribe of Siberia. In this wonderful place, the White Youth sees a mighty hill, and on the hill an immense tree. The resin of this tree is transparent and sweetly perfumed; its bark never dries or cracks, its leaves never wither, and liquid light flows through all its branches. These branches pierce the sky, penetrating the 'nine spheres and seven storeys of heaven'. Its very top is the tethering-post for the supreme god, Ai-Toyon. Its roots, like Yggdrasil's, penetrate into the underworld, where they become the pillars of strange mythical beings. Through the rustling of its leaves the tree converses with the spirits of the sky-world.

As the White Youth looks at it, these leaves begin to rustle, a fine white rain falls from them, and a warm breeze blows. The tree begins to shrink, creaking and groaning as it does so. From within it, there appears a spirit, an ancient white-haired goddess, 'as gaily coloured as a partridge, and with breasts as large as leather bags'. The White Youth, or Lonely Man, as he is sometimes called, addresses the tree-divinity. 'High Honoured Mistress', he says, 'Spirit of my tree and of my dwelling place, everything living moves in couples, and gives birth to descendants, but I am alone. I wish to travel and seek a partner worthy of me. I wish to know others and measure my strength against them. I wish to live as a man should. Do not refuse thy blessing, I pray thee, with humbled, bowed head and bent knees.'

He now learns from the divinity that his mother is Kubaichotum, the mother of all things, and his father is the celestial god Ai-Toyon. They lowered him from heaven that he might become the ancestor of mankind. The tree goddess then takes water from under the root of the tree, and pouring it into a bladder gives it to him, saying, 'Bind this under thy left arm; it will bring thee salvation in extremity.' (Later in the same tale, the hero fights a duel with a dragon, and receives a fatal blow in the heart, but as the bladder bursts his heart is immediately whole again.) Finally, the goddess blesses him, and offers him milk from her ample breasts: as he drinks he feels his strength grow ninefold.

This gaily coloured, full-breasted tree divinity is one of the many epiphanies or divine manifestations of the Great Mother Goddess known to mythology the world over. As the Earth Mother (Tellus Mater), 'Mother-of-all-Things', she embodies the regenerative powers contained within the earth and the waters. It is out of her watery depths that all life emerges, and in her caves and crevices that all potential life resides. Hers is the teeming womb of life, able endlessly to absorb and reabsorb, to create and regenerate, a perpetual source of cosmic fertility.

Woman and Tree alike embody this Great Earth Mother, for both are visible manifestations of her fruitfulness (pls. 10, 11, 13). In the Yakut myth, the White Youth discovers in the vicinity of the great tree, perhaps surrounding the hill on which it stood, 'a lake of milk, with curdled swamps at its shores'. What more powerful image could one find for the maternal waters from which all things arose, and, in which they continue to have their being? This is the milk of the Great Goddess herself, the essential life-giving liquid which swells the breasts of women and flows as sap through every tree. In India this life-sap is called Soma or Amrita, and is the heavenly elixir or 'water of life' from which the gods obtain immortality. It is the innermost essence of all the life-giving liquids (water, blood, semen, milk, sap) which flow throughout the cosmos, ensuring the regeneration of all life.

For archaic man, the annual death and rebirth of nature was a great mystery drama, whose meaning was celebrated in his myths and rituals. In winter everything was seen to return to its dark origins in the womb of the Earth Mother. In spring, the primordial act, the original creation of the cosmos, was repeated anew. In the ancient world this event was celebrated as the *hieros gamos* – the holy marriage – of the Earth Mother and her son and lover, the god of vegetation. Every spring he was born anew in plant and tree, in summer flourishing to full maturity, only to enter her again in the autumn, to fertilize her with his 'ripened seed' in the great cosmic night of winter.

About 4000 BC, the ancient Mesopotamians tell how the goddess Ishtar goes in search of her young son-lover, because his absence is causing widespread desolation and grief in the land of the living. In the ancient Babylonian hymns he is likened to the fading tamarisk and willow. Around the seventh century before Christ, the Greeks adopted his worship, calling him Adonis (meaning Lord). They said that he had been born of a myrrh tree, the bark of which had burst after a ten-month gestation (pl. 18).

The Egyptians also had a vegetation god whose myth has come down to us from Plutarch and the Pyramid texts. It tells how the divine king Osiris ruled over Egypt, with his sister-spouse Isis. In the twenty-eighth year of his reign his wicked brother Set trapped him in a wooden coffer, which he threw into the Nile. This coffer eventually landed at Byblos, on the eastern shore of the Mediterranean.

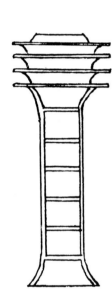

Here a beautiful erica-tree grew up, enclosing the coffer in its trunk. The king of Byblos, admiring the tree, had it made into a pillar for his palace. In the meantime, the wandering and grief-stricken Isis arrived in search of Osiris. On seeing the pillar she immediately recognized what it contained, and begged it from the king. Her wish was granted, and she removed the coffer, leaving the tree pillar behind to be worshipped by the people of Byblos. Later in the story, when Isis is away, the wicked Set comes upon the coffer whilst he is out hunting. Recognizing the body, he cuts it into pieces and scatters them through the length and breadth of Egypt. After much further searching, Isis finally recovers all the pieces with the vital exception of the phallus, which has, significantly, re-entered the earth, descending to the depths of the ocean in the body of a fish. Isis, aided by the magic arts of her sister Nephthys, makes an image of it, and with this, and the other pieces restores the body of Osiris to an everlasting life in the Egyptian afterworld, where he weighs the hearts of the dead, to determine whether they too should receive the rewards of immortality.

An important Egyptian symbol is associated with the immortal Osiris. This is the Djed Pillar, which became the hieroglyph for 'duration and stability'. The Djed Pillar derived originally from the image of the tree with lopped-off branches. But what is especially interesting is that this original tree-image was fused with an image of Osiris' sacrum, the lowest joint of the backbone. This part of the dismembered Osiris was believed to be the immortal seat of the god's virility. Its position at the base of the spine corresponds significantly to the 'root-chakra' of Indian yoga, where Kundalini, the vital energy, resides.

In ancient Rome, the great Spring Festival celebrated the *hieros gamos* of the Asiatic fertility goddess Cybele and her youthful lover, the shepherd Attis. Attis was the son of the virgin Nana, who had conceived him by ingesting a ripe almond, seed of the tree that heralds the Spring by flowering long before its leaves open. The myth tells that Cybele loved Attis so passionately that she made him emasculate himself so that he could belong to none but her. He did this beneath a pine tree, in which his spirit resided after he had bled to death.

In Rome on 22 March, a pine tree was cut and brought into the sanctuary of Cybele, where it was swathed like a corpse with woollen bands and decked with wreaths of violets; for violets were said to have sprung from the blood of Attis. To its stem his effigy was tied, and then it was taken in solemn procession to the temple. The next day a strict fast was observed in preparation for the celebration of the Day of Blood (Dies Sanguinis) on 24 March. On this day there was a ritual re-enactment of the death of Attis. Amid much wailing and lamentation, the effigy was removed and buried in a tomb, while the priests of Cybele gashed their arms in remembrance of his sacrifice. (In the original Phrygian rite, the initiates had actually emasculated themselves and their severed parts had been ritually buried in the earth.) After a night of vigil and fasting the tomb was opened and found to be empty, and the longed-for message was proclaimed: 'Neophytes, be of good cheer. The god is saved. We also after our toils shall find salvation.' From that moment, sorrow turned to joy, and the day was known as Hilaria, the Festival of Joy, when universal licence prevailed.

This Festival of Joy recalls the celebrations of European folk communities, when the people actively participated in the resurrection of the plant world. In spring or early summer, or Midsummer's day, it was, and still is in some parts of Europe, the custom to go out into the woods, cut down a fir tree, and bring it into the village, where it is stripped and decorated just as the tree of Attis was. J. G. Frazer, in *The Golden Bough*, quotes an entertaining description of these festivities in rural England, by the Elizabethan puritan Phillip Stubbes. He describes, with much disgust, how they used to bring in the May, in the days of Good Queen Bess.

'Against May, Whitsonday, or other time, all the yung men and maides, olde men and wives, run gadding over night to the woods, groves, hils, and mountains, where they spend all the night in plesant pastimes; and in the morning they return, bringing with them birch and branches of trees, to deck their assemblies withall. And no mervaile, for there is a great Lord present among them, as superintendent and Lord over their pastimes and sportes, namely, Sathan, prince of Hel. But the chiefest jewel they bring from hence is their May-pole, which they bring home with great veneration, as thus. They have twentie or fortie yoke of oxen, every oxe having a sweet nosegay of flouers placed on the tip of his hornes, and these oxen drawe home this May-pole (this stinkyng ydol, rather), which is covered all over with floures and herbs, bound round about with strings, from the top to the bottom, and sometime painted with variable colours, with two or three hundred men, women and children following it with great devotion. And thus beeing reared up, with handkercheefs and flags hovering on the top, they straw the ground rounde about, binde green boughs about it, set up sommer haules, bowers, and arbors hard by it. And then fall they to dance about it, like as the heathen people did at the dedication of the Idols, whereof this is a perfect pattern, or rather the thing itself. I have heard it credibly reported (and that *viva voce*) by men of great gravitie and reputation, that of fortie, threescore, or a hundred maides going to the wood over night, there have scaresly the third part of them returned home again undefiled.'

The Tree of Ascent

The transformation of the tree into a pillar or pole brings about a shift of symbolic meaning. The foliage is that part of the tree which responds to change. Stripping the tree of this foliage reveals its changeless centre; the vertical axis around which the visible world of the tree revolves. For the cosmic tree reflects not only the endless regeneration of the cosmos but also its undying centre. At the spring festivals the tree is stripped of its foliage because at that time the re-creation of the cosmos is celebrated and its source is revealed. Through the dance around the maypole, and in the intertwining of the bands, the dancers actively participate in creation, the weaving of the world; the bands and the flowers parallel the decoration of the ancient Attis tree.

The Maypole is the cosmic pole, the Axis Mundi, which instead of branching, leafing and flowering out into the world, *centres* on the Pole Star, around which the heavens revolve. From here it descends, to become the axis of the world.

Such a central axis, in the form of a pillar or smoke-hole, is a characteristic of many 'primitive' dwellings. Here the same symbolism pertains, for these human structures are made in imitation of the cosmos, a cosmos created, structured and sanctified by the gods. That a central axis is the single most important feature of all dwelling, even under the open sky, is tragically illustrated at the most archaic level of culture, by a story concerning one of the clans of the Arunta, an Aboriginal tribe of Central Australia. A sacred pole always stood at the centre of their world; for after creating the world in mythical times, their creator god Numbakula fashioned such a pole out of a gum tree, and then climbed up it to the sky-world, never to be seen again. The clan carried an imitation of this pole with them on their wanderings, travelling always in the direction it seemed to point. The ethnologists Spencer and Gillen record that once this pole got broken, and that, after wandering for some time quite aimlessly, the entire clan lay down to die. Life for them no longer seemed worth living, for the axis of their world was broken and communication with the sacred lost.

Ascents and descents into sky and underworld are a central feature of shamanism. This is the name given to the religion of those peoples whose spiritual life centres around a shaman (pl. 60) – a particular type of religious ecstatic, who combines the roles of mystic, visionary, healer, artist, poet and magician. Shamanism has its own symbolic structure, which it retains even when it combines, as it has often done, with other religious forms (including Buddhism and Christianity). The evidence of the painted caves suggests that it was the religion of the hunters of Palaeolithic times. In modern times, its purest form has been found in the polar regions, and especially among the tribes of Siberia and Central Asia. It spread from these regions to other parts of Asia, to Oceania, and across the Bering Straits to the Americas. The shaman is vitally important to his community, though set apart from it; for he is in direct communication with the spirit world, which he enters regularly in religious ecstasy and trance. In this condition he attains to the 'centre of the world', for it is only through this centre that he can penetrate the spirit world.

Thus, when the need arises, the Altaic shamans of Siberia perform their ritual ascent to the sky world: this is done from time to time for every family, and continues for two to three consecutive evenings. On the first, the shaman places a young birch tree, stripped of its lower branches, at the centre of a specially constructed skin tent or *yurt*. The roof of this represents the vault of the sky, through which the few remaining branches protrude. Nine notches are cut into the trunk of this tree; these represent the nine heavens through which the shaman will pass in his ritual ascent. A light-coloured horse is then chosen for sacrifice; on the soul of this horse the shaman will ride throughout his celestial journey. Next, the shaman invokes the spirits inviting them to enter into his drum. On this drum, the shaman will also ride, for it is his prolonged drumming that summons and concentrates the energies he needs to enter the spiritual world. This drum is the shaman's single most important possession. Its wooden frame is understood to have been made from a branch that the supreme god, Bai Ulgen, let fall from the Cosmic Tree. It is up this tree that it will carry him; for on the next evening the most important part of the ceremony begins, a lengthy ritual in the course of which, in mounting ecstasy, the shaman symbolically climbs the birch. As he raises himself by degrees upon its notches, he sings:

> *I have climbed a step,*
> *I have reached a plane,*

and then, on ascending further,

> *I have broken through the second ground,*
> *I have climbed the second level,*
> *See, the ground lies in splinters.*

He then continues to climb, with various stops on the way, during which he relates extraordinary adventures and episodes concerning the various beings that he meets. Thus, he passes from heaven to heaven, through to the ninth or even to the twelfth. When he has gone as high as his power permits, he meets and converses with Bai Ulgen, receiving predictions concerning the weather and the future harvest. After this, the culmination of his ecstasy, he collapses exhausted, remaining motionless and speechless for some time. Eventually he wakes, rubbing his eyes, and greets those present as though after a long absence.

For the Navaho of the American South-West, the Axis Mundi is a reed, through the centre of which their mythical ancestors crawled as they progressed through the four subterranean worlds that lie beneath this one. Their origin myth, a myth of emergence like that of their neighbours the Zuñí, tells how the ancestors were forced by a series of natural disasters, flooding, overcrowding and disease, from one under-world to another, each one an improvement on the last. Each of these underworlds is dominated by a single colour and by a particular species of animal and plant. It is only in this world, the fifth, that all the colours and natural species come together, bringing to birth the fullness of light and colour, man and the world. But, according to the Navaho myths, all is not yet complete. Man himself still needs further trans-formation; and so the Axis Mundi continues to climb. In the Navaho sandpaintings (pl. 5) it is pictured as a giant corn-plant through the centre of which runs the 'path of blessing' or 'sacred pollen-path', image for the life path of Man. It is up this path that the Navaho twin culture heroes, Monster-Slayer and Reared-in-the-Earth, followed the Axis Mundi through various sky-worlds to the house of their heavenly father the sun. It was here, the myths tell, that they had to undergo a severe initiation, an ordeal by fire and water. Only after this did they receive the sun's blessing and return to earth with knowledge of the sacred art of sandpainting.

The Navaho make these sandpaintings as part of the elaborate ceremonials or 'chantways' in which they symbolically re-enact the events of mythical times. The structure of the paintings is always symmetrical and centres around some symbol of the Axis Mundi. This centredness and symmetry is especially significant, since the chief purpose of the paintings is therapeutic (see p. 100). At a certain point in the pro-ceedings the patient is actually placed upon the painting, and sand from the figures is applied to his body. The purpose of this action is to plunge him, psychologically and spiritually, into mythical time and space. This is a dimension stronger and more vital than that of profane, everyday existence, because it is the time and space in which things *first* came to be. It is this experience of a 'return to origins', at the axial centre of the world, that integrates the patient and effects the cure.

The Inverted Tree

The idea of the cosmic tree as imperishably fixed in the empyrean is also expressed in the image of the inverted tree, with its roots above and its branches below. This image appears in widely different traditions. For instance one finds it used in the rituals of the Aborigine shamans of Australia, and among the Lapps, who, when sacrificing to the god of vegetation, placed an inverted tree beside their altar. Why they did this can perhaps be best understood by exploring the explicit meaning of this image in two of the world's 'higher' religions.

The inverted tree is described in the earliest Indian scriptures – the Vedas and Upanishads (*c.* 900–500 BC). The *Katha Upanishad* describes it thus: 'This eternal asvattha whose roots rise on high and whose branches grow low is the pure, the Brahman, what is called Non-Death. All the worlds rest in it.' Here, the asvattha, a fig tree, represents the manifestation of the cosmos from a single transcendent source, Brahman; and creation is seen as a descending movement. 'The threefold Brahman has its root above,' says the *Maitreya Upanishad*, refering to the three main stems of the cosmic tree. These represent the Hindu Trinity, the three gods of the cosmic process; Brahma, god of Creation, Vishnu, god of Preservation, and Shiva, god of Dissolution. From these three, further branchings occur, for each, with his female consort, has actively participated, through different incarnations, in the cycles of time and history. Through the image of the inverted tree, Indian metaphysics subtly reconciles Hindu polytheism with the monotheistic viewpoint. For all these gods and goddesses are the manifold branchings of a single, hidden root.

Apart from the asvattha (pipal tree, *Ficus religiosa*), with its heart-shaped leaves, another oval-leafed fig tree is equally venerated in India. This is the nyagrodha or banyan tree (*Ficus indica*), which has the peculiar habit of growing on other trees. Its seeds are deposited, by birds and other animals, high up in the branches of forest trees. From these they send down long aerial roots, which touch the ground and grow up again. As they do so they weave a curious basketwork around the trunk of the host tree, until it finally dies away, leaving the vigorous banyan in its stead (pl. 64). While it is the asvattha that is most often referred to in the Indian scriptures, it was the banyan, with its long aerial roots, which provided the underlying image of the inverted tree. Its natural action reflected the vigorous manifestations of the sacred throughout the cosmos, from a single and transcendent source, the 'seed' of Brahman.

It was this same mysterious relationship, between the invisible, transcendent God and the visible world of Creation, that haunted medieval Jewish mysticism, and most especially that form of it known as the Kabbalah. The Kabbalists understood creation to be the outward manifestation of the inner world of God, and they used the image of the inverted tree to exemplify this idea (pl. 38). For, just as the seed contains the tree, and the tree the seed, so the hidden world of God contains all Creation, and Creation is, in turn, a revelation of the hidden world of God. Thus, in the *Book of Bahir*, the oldest known Kabbalistic text, written around 1180 in southern France, we read: 'All the divine powers form a succession of layers and are like a tree.' And in the most influential Kabbalistic text of all, the thirteenth-century *Book of Zohar* (by Moses of León), one finds: 'Now the Tree of Life extends from above downwards, and is the sun which illuminates all.'

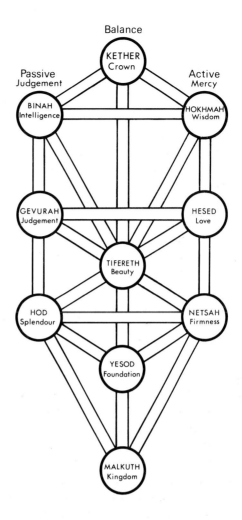

To describe God's latency the Kabbalists used the combined images of the seed ('Hidden Seed'), the root ('Root of all Roots') and the mathematical point ('Primordial or Smooth Point'). The association of 'Primordial Point' and 'Hidden Seed' is especially significant, since we shall meet it in an important modern context later. This is how the *Book of Zohar* describes the beginning of creation:

'When the Concealed of the Concealed wished to reveal himself, he first made a single point: the Infinite was entirely unknown, and diffused no light before this luminous point broke through into vision.

'Beyond this point nothing is knowable, and that is why it is called *reshith*, beginning, the first of those creative words by which the universe was created.'

This first revelation of God's inwardness proceeds by a series of ten divine emanations, called the Sephiroth, the spheres of God. These Sephiroth represent the divine attributes, powers and potencies, and are arranged in groups of three to form the Kabbalistic Tree of Life. There are three vertical columns: the Pillar of Judgment, consisting of Binah (Intelligence), Din or Gevurah (Judgment), and Hod (Splendour); the Pillar of Mercy, consisting of Hokhmah (Wisdom), Hesed (Love) and Netsah (Firmness); and between them the reconciling column, the Middle Pillar, sometimes called the Balance, consisting of Kether (Crown), Rahamin (Compassion) or Tifereth (Beauty), Yesod (Foundation) and Malkuth (Kingdom). These also read across to form the three interdependent worlds of Intellect (Kether, Binah, Hokhmah), Imagination (Din, Hesed, Tifereth, Hod, Netsah and sometimes Yesod) and Matter (Yesod and Malkuth). There is, further, a sexual symbolism evolved in the web of relationships between these ten Sephiroth, for each represents a masculine and active or a feminine and passive potency of God. Finally, this mystical Tree links the three worlds of God, Man and Universe, for it reveals the inner workings of all three. Man and the Universe are each a reflection of the other, and both are a reflection of the boundless infinity of what the Kabbalists called En-Sof, the Endless; that impersonal 'god beyond God' which human finite consciousness cannot reach, but in which both Man and the World are mysteriously plunged.

An important (and perhaps better-known) Jewish symbol related to the cosmic tree is the seven-branched candlestick known as the menorah. Its biblical origin is to be found in Exodus (25:31–40), where Moses is instructed by God to make a menorah as one of the chief objects of the Tabernacle. It is to be made of one piece, out of pure beaten gold, according to the divine pattern shown to Moses on the mountain. This was the model for the golden menorah which eventually stood in the Temple in Jerusalem (pl. 52). The form of the menorah derived, like so many other forms of the cosmic tree, from ancient Mesopotamia. Its seven branches originated in the astrological significance of the number seven, which stood for the seven heavenly bodies known at that time (Sun, Moon, Mercury, Venus, Mars, Jupiter and Saturn). For the great Jewish philosopher Philo of Alexandria (c. 30 BC–AD 50), whose ambition was to unite the Mosaic Law and Oriental thought with the Greek philosophy of Plato, the branched arcs of the lampstand represented the paths of the planets around the Sun, represented by the 'fixed' vertical centre shaft, whose lamp was the Light of God from which the other six derived their reflected glory. The pattern shown to Moses upon the mountain was the inner spiritual form of the cosmos, of which the menorah was the outer reflection. The seven menorah lamps were also the seven 'eyes of the Lord', seen by the prophet Zechariah in his vision of the golden lampstand (Zechariah 4). This stood between two olive trees which provided the oil for the lamps. This particular association is also found in the Koran (ch. 24), where 'an olive that is neither of the East nor of the West' (i.e. at the 'centre of the world') would burn 'even if no fire touched it'.

The Tree of Sacrifice

Modern historians think it highly unlikely that Christ was crucified on an actual cross. It was much more likely a simple stake, the cross being shaped more by the action of myth than that of history. For the earliest Christians it was the cosmic significance of Christ's sacrifice which gave the historical event on Calvary its meaning; a meaning which was expressed through the symbol of the Cross. Christ is sacrificed at the centre of the world, on the Cosmic Tree, which stretches from heaven to earth and stands at the midpoint of the horizontal radial cross of the four directions. This Cross is homologized with the Tree of Life, which according to the scriptures stands at the centre of the Garden of Eden at the beginning of time and at the centre of the Heavenly City of Jerusalem at the end of time. In the third century, this image of the Cosmic Cross of Christ was beautifully evoked in an Easter sermon by Hippolytus, Bishop of Rome.

'This tree, wide as the heavens itself, has grown up into heaven from the earth. It is an immortal growth and towers between heaven and earth. It is the fulcrum of all things and the place where they are all at rest. It is the foundation of the round world, the centre of the cosmos. In it all the diversities in our human nature are formed into a unity. It is held together by the invisible nails of the spirit so that it may not break loose from the divine. It touches the highest summits of heaven and makes the earth firm beneath its foot, and it grasps the middle regions between them with immeasurable arms.'

The Christian attributes of spiritual and temporal power all participate in this cosmic symbolism. The royal orb is an image of the world with the cosmic cross at the centre, and the royal sceptre and the bishop's crozier, which are often represented as a living branch, invest the holder with the centrality and power pertaining to the Tree of Life which grows at the Centre. When the coronation mantle, with the Tree of Life embroidered upon it, was placed upon the shoulders of the Holy Roman Emperor, and when the Patriarch of Venice sat on the Throne of St Mark, with the Tree of Life and the four rivers of Paradise carved on its back, each was placed symbolically at that supremely sacred place, the centre of the world (see pp. 102–03).

At the most archaic levels of culture, elementary forms of sacred place constitute a cosmos in miniature. They most often consist of a landscape of trees, stone and water, as with the totem centres of the Australian Aborigines, or else of a sacred enclosure containing altar, stone and tree, such as might be found in some parts of India to this day. At the time when Buddha was preaching in India (c. 563–483 BC), such sacrificial altars set up for the popular worship of the fertility divinities (Yaksas) were to be found in profusion. And it was upon such an altar beneath a sacred banyan tree that the future Buddha chose to sit when he sacrificed his selfhood and achieved enlightenment. The Tree under which he sat became the holy Bo or Bodhi Tree, the Tree of Enlightenment, a cutting of which still grows and is venerated at Bodh Gaya (pl. 27).

The Buddhist legends tell how the Buddha, having finally arrived at a thorough understanding of the finite limitations and conditions of existence, resolved to transcend them through renunciation. He resolved that, though his bones would waste away and his blood dry up, he would not leave his seat beneath the sacred banyan tree until he had successfully transcended the conditions of existence and broken through to an immediate realization of the Ultimate and Unconditioned Truth (Bodhi). The Buddha's struggle for enlightenment, which is said to have taken forty-nine days, is pictured mythologically as the Temptation and Assault of Kama-Mara, demonic lord of the cosmic process. First he appeared as Kama (Desire), with his three beautiful daughters, who sang and danced before the Buddha, using every means in their power to arouse his passion and desire. Then, having failed in this, he appeared as Mara (Death) with his infernal hosts. Amid storms of wind and rain and volcanic eruptions of boiling mud and lava, monstrous beings assaulted him with rocks and uprooted trees. While this was happening the earth tipped giddily in each of the four directions, but every time it righted itself, and the infernal missiles turned to flowers as they entered the Buddha's field of concentration. For the Buddha remained immovably fixed at the centre: spiritually, he was one with the axis of the universe; symbolically, he had climbed the Cosmic Tree and was viewing the antics of Kama-Mara from another plane. This is one of the reasons why in the earliest Buddhist representations of this event the Buddha himself is never portrayed. He had transcended the level on which these events took place. Having achieved enlightenment he was no longer subject to the limitations and conditions of existence; being one with the inner being of the whole cosmos, he is more truly represented by the image of the Cosmic Tree itself. Furthermore, the Tree, with its spreading subterranean roots, narrow trunk and spreading foliage, is a perfect image for the actual process of enlightenment: for the raising, channelling and concentration of the latent energies required for spiritual transformation. This is why in the earliest Buddhist texts it is the Bodhi Tree, and not the Buddha, that is referred to as the Great Awakener.

It was around a sacred tree or pole that the North American Indians performed many of their rituals to strengthen relations with the sacred world. The most famous of these is the sun dance. Black Elk gives an account of this rite among the Sioux in his book *The Sacred Pipe*, where he tells of the sacred origin of the rite: how it came to one of the braves in a vision, and how it was first performed.

In an elaborate ritual a sacred cottonwood tree is felled and brought ceremonially into the camp. This tree becomes the centre pole for the sacred sun dance lodge. Twenty-eight poles radiate from it; these represent the twenty-eight phases of the lunar month. 'We are really making the universe in a likeness,' says Black Elk, 'for each of the posts around the lodge represents some particular object of creation, so that the whole circle is the entire creation, and the one tree at the centre upon which the twenty-eight poles rest is Wakan-Tanka – the Great Spirit, who is the centre of everything.'

After the construction of this cosmic house, eight of the bravest warriors are chosen and painted with sacred symbols: the circle, the cross, the sun and moon and morning star. They then put on rabbit skins to make them docile and to help them accept their sufferings in a spirit of humility – 'a quality we must all possess when we go to the centre of the world'. Then, after more prayers and sacred vows, they circumambulate the sacred lodge in a sunwise direction, crying out: 'O Wakan-Tanka, be merciful to me, that my people may live! It is for this that I am sacrificing myself.'

The breast of each dancer is then pierced in two places by wooden pegs, which are attached to a leather thong, which is tied to the upper part of the centre pole. When the dance begins, each warrior in turn leans back upon the thongs, which represent 'rays of light from Wakan-Tanka', and dances around the pole until the pegs break loose from his flesh. The ritual ends with each of the dancers placing a piece of his severed flesh at the base of the tree, while the following prayer is addressed to the Great Spirit. 'These eight people have offered their bodies and souls to you; in suffering they have sent their voices to you; they have even offered to you a piece of their flesh, which is now at the foot of this sacred tree. The favour that they ask of you is that their people may walk in holy path of life and that they may increase in sacred manner.'

Finally, the dancers are addressed: 'By your actions you have strengthened the sacred hoop of our nation. You have made a closer relationship with all the things of the universe.' Black Elk concludes: 'A great thing had been done, and in the winters to come much strength would be given to the life of the nation through this rite.'

It was from the great World Tree, Yggdrasil, that stood at the centre of the three cosmic regions, that the Nordic god Odin hung and suffered for nine days and nights. In the Eddic poem known as the *Havamal* (The Utterance of the High One), Odin says:

I know that I hung
On the windswept Tree
Nine days and nights.
I was struck with a spear
And given to Odin,
Myself to myself.

It was once thought that this image of the suffering god hanging on the tree was the result of late Christian influences on Nordic mythology. But this interpretation is now discounted because of the many parallels that have been found with the shamanic symbolism of Northern and Central Asia. For example, we have seen how the Siberian shamans sacrifice a horse, upon whose soul they ride in their ecstatic ascent to the sky-world. Now, one of the names of Odin was Ygg, and the name of the World Tree, Ygg-drasil, means 'steed of Odin'. Furthermore, the top of the tree was referred to as the tethering-post of the god. Finally, in Nordic tradition (pl. 51) the gibbet was called the 'hanged man's horse', and ritual hangings played a significant part in the cult of Odin.

Odin's sacrifice of his self to his self was made to gain the wisdom of the magic runes, which represent the secret language of the other world, or of the sacred.

They helped me neither
By meat nor drink.
I peered downward,
I took up the runes,
Screaming, I took them –
Then I fell back.

Odin's suffering is akin to the initiatory suffering of the Siberian shamans, in whose myths and rituals the World Tree plays such a significant part. At the onset of their mystical vocation, future shamans quite often suffer an involuntary illness, during which they may remain unconscious for several days. During this period the future shaman undergoes the most important part of his initiation, which he experiences in the form of a dream. It is only after this personal initiation that he is instructed in the traditional techniques by an older shaman of the tribe.

The Russian ethnographer A. A. Popov recorded the initiatory dream of a Samoyed shaman, and this is one of the examples cited by Eliade in his book on shamanism. This shaman dreamt that his soul was carried off to a great sea, in the middle of which was an island, and in the centre of the island a huge tree. Among the branches of this tree (which is, of course, the Tree of the World) he saw the shaman ancestors of many different nations. He then heard voices telling him that he was to have a drum made from a branch of this tree. From the Lord of the Tree, who emerged in human form, he received his branch, along with all the other shamans in the tree. The Lord of the Tree then said: 'One branch only I give not to the shamans, for I keep it for the rest of mankind. They can make dwellings from it and so use it for their needs. I am the Tree that gives life to all men.'

After this, the shaman flew on, clasping his branch, and after further adventures, came to the opening ăt the base of a mountain. Looking inside, he saw his own body being cut to pieces and placed in a great cauldron, where it was boiled for three years. After this, the parts of his body were removed and reforged piece by piece on three giant anvils. Last of all, the blacksmith reforged his head, giving him new 'mystical' eyes, and piercing his ears, so that he could read the letters inside his head and understand the language of animals and plants.

This is one of many examples cited by Eliade to show how the shaman's sensibility is changed by his initiatory experiences. For after these the shaman is gifted with paranormal powers – clairvoyance, clairaudience, and the ability to enter and return from the trance state at will – and it is to these that he owes his ability to shamanize. The shaman's sufferings, like Odin's, enable him to understand the language of the other world: passing beyond the normal confines of the human condition, he can ascend and descend at will into those regions where the souls of the sick involuntarily stray.

The Tree of Knowledge

Besides the Tree of Life there was another tree in Paradise: the Tree of the Knowledge of Good and Evil. In Genesis (2:17) God forbids Adam and Eve to eat the fruit of this tree, telling them that if they do so they will surely die. The serpent, however, tempts Eve to eat the fruit, telling her that it is forbidden because God knows 'that in the day ye eat thereof, then shall your eyes be opened, and ye shall be as Gods, knowing good and evil' (Genesis 3:5). Adam and Eve then eat, their eyes are opened, and they *know* for the first time that they are naked. Because of their disobedience God expels them from the garden, cursing them and telling them that in the future they will have to work by the sweat of their brows, 'till thou return unto the ground, for out of it thou wast taken; for dust thou art and unto dust thou shalt return'. God then sets an angel with a flaming sword at the gates of Paradise to guard 'the way of the Tree of Life' in case they take also of this, 'and eat, and live forever' (Genesis 3:24).

The theme of the two trees is not confined to Judaism and Christianity. The ancient Babylonians had two trees, the Tree of Truth and the Tree of Life, at the eastern entry to heaven. In the Hawaiian Islands these two, the tree of eternal life and the tree which brings knowledge of death, are pictured as one. For the natives of these islands the entrances to the land of the dead were clefts in the earth. These were called 'casting-off places'. In one of their myths the soul arriving at such a place finds a tree with a group of little children gathered around it. One side of this tree is alive and green, the other dead, dry and brittle. The children instruct the soul to climb the brittle side and then descend the other in order to grasp a *living* branch which will break, and hurl it into the 'labyrinth that leads to the underworld'.

Here, as in Genesis, there is a paradox. The little children surrounding the Hawaiian tree are the souls of the unborn; they represent the state of unfulfilled perfection, like the 'dreaming innocence' of Adam before the Fall. But, as the modern theologian Paul Tillich has pointed out, this state of potentiality is not perfection, though Christianity has often tried to call it so. For the actualization of perfection there must first be a fall into disobedience and sin. In the biblical story it is the woman Eve's acceptance of the subtle wisdom of the serpent which brings about this necessary fall. She is responsible for Adam's second birth, into the world. The trees can be seen, in Tillich's terms, as the two temptations or anxieties between which man stands: 'the anxiety of losing himself by not actualizing himself and the anxiety of losing himself by actualizing himself and his potentialities. He stands between the preservation of his dreaming innocence without experiencing the actuality of being and the loss of his innocence through knowledge, power and guilt. The anxiety of this situation is the state of temptation. Man decides for self-actualization, thus producing the end of dreaming innocence.'

Like Adam, man grasps the fruit of finite freedom and experience, accepting the fear and guilt that accompany any act of independent self-realization. Before the Fall, Adam and Eve ate the fruits of the Tree of Life unknowingly; after the Fall, they taste the bitter-sweet fruits of the Tree of Knowledge of Good and Evil, which eventually becomes, through Christ's example, the redemptive Tree of Suffering and Salvation. In Blake's painting of the Fall (pl. 45), it is Christ himself, the incarnate son of the Transcendent God, who leads them out of the Garden of Innocence into the World of Experience, to follow the long path of suffering and sin, the Via Dolorosa, that will ultimately lead them to fulfilment.

In myth, folklore and fairytale, and in traditional iconography, one often finds serpents or fabulous beasts mounting guard over symbolic equivalents for the spiritual 'treasure that is hard to attain' – as in the legend of St George, or in that of Hercules' quest for the golden apples of the tree of the Hesperides. For, while any object in the cosmos can reveal the presence of the sacred, it is only by succeeding in the difficult task of mastering the vital forces, symbolized by the 'animal powers', that the hero can gain personal access to the sacred realm itself (pl. 3).

What is described at the popular level in these myths and legends is 'internalized' in meditative techniques and spiritual disciplines like Yoga. Thus, in Kundalini Yoga, the human body is conceived as a microcosm, the axis of which is the spinal column. The life force, closely allied with sexuality, is imagined as the serpent Kundalini, which sleeps coiled at the base of the 'spinal tree'. The task of the yogi is to arouse this sleeping force and get it to climb the spinal tree, piercing the various spiritual centres (chakras) on its way, until finally it is released from the Sahasrara Chakra, the Thousand-petalled Lotus, at the top of the head. At this point the heavy material forces of the earth and the waters, embodied in the snake, take flight; struggling ascent becomes transcendent flight. The mythical eagle Garuda carries off Kundalini in its beak; heaven and earth, light and darkness, spirit and flesh are finally, ecstatically united. The difficult ascent of the spinal tree is imagined as a twofold path winding between opposites symbolizing the tragic ambiguities and dynamic polarities of life (see p. 113). At different levels of experience, symbolized by the ascending chakras, these contraries are resolved: the paths cross, and a breakthrough in the level of consciousness is achieved. This motif of the intertwining serpents is an archetypal model for the process of spiritual and psychological growth. It is also to be found in our own Western spiritual tradition as the Caduceus, the staff of Hermes, healer of souls, messenger of the gods and master of the Hermetic art of alchemy.

Most people know that alchemy, whose origin lies in the metallurgical practices of the ancient and primitive worlds, was the forerunner of the physical science of chemistry. What is perhaps less well known is that it is also the forerunner of modern depth psychology. At least, that is how Carl Gustav Jung, one of the pioneers of the psychology of the unconscious, understood it. He felt that the strange symbolic language of the old alchemists could teach us much about the nature of the psyche. In his great book *Psychology and Alchemy*, Jung shows how the alchemist's attempt to transmute base metal into gold is the outer manifestation of an inner process whose real goal is the transformation of himself. The whole alchemical Magnum Opus or

Great Work, the crucibles, flasks and furnaces, the elemental powers of earth, air, fire and water, the metals with their astrological significations, the processes of blackening, whitening, yellowing and reddening, of calcination, conjunction, putrefaction, solution, and coagulation, are all outer reflections of inner psychic forces through which the alchemist seeks the transmutation of his own soul.

Jung saw a correlation between the alchemical process and what he called the process of individuation. Exploring the structure of the unconscious over a long period, by scrupulously following the spontaneous imagery of dreams, both his own and his patients', Jung discovered that they followed a pattern akin to that of natural and organic growth. Psychological development proceeds generally in a spiral pattern. During the course of life dreams seem to 'circumambulate a centre', revolving around a hidden core of meaning and turning the attention of the dreamer to the same or similar problems always at a deeper and a higher level of understanding than before. As this process develops, it gradually gives rise to a dawning awareness of that unity of being, which, following the example of Indian metaphysics, Jung calls the Self. This gradual shift of centre from the ego to a deeper and broader sense of Self takes place by means of a dialogue between the ego, with its consciously held values, and the archetypal images which arise from the deepest collective levels of the unconscious, shared by all men. These recurring images in dreams and fantasies resemble, to an amazing degree, the mythical images of ancient and 'primitive' cultures.

This process of Self-realization is frequently represented in dreams by centred and symmetrical images, those images of polarity and wholeness which Jung calls mandalas. One which frequently appears in dreams, often in a strangely symbolic and archaic form, is the Tree. Jung interprets it as a 'symbol of the Self in cross section . . . the Self depicted as a process of growth'. For the alchemists it symbolizes the alchemical process itself in the form of the *arbor philosophica* (pl. 39), which the adept might well have 'seen' as he gazed through the misty and reflective glass of his alchemical flask.

'I pray you look with the eyes of the mind at the little tree of the grain of wheat, regarding all its circumstances, so that you may bring the tree of the philosophers to grow,' writes one seventeenth-century alchemist; thus projecting on to nature the inner image of his own transformation. His words are echoed three centuries later by another who instinctively understood this process, the German poet Rainer Maria Rilke, who wrote:

> *Oh, I who long to grow,*
> *I look outside myself, and the tree*
> *inside me grows.*

The alchemists' perfecting of themselves went hand in hand with the redemption of the whole of nature, which was seen as the eventual realization of the *ultima materia*, that state of ultimate perfection that was potentially present in the *materia prima* or primordial matter with which the Great Work began. They conceived of the metallic ores as maturing and gestating in the earth, and felt that they were hastening this cosmic process in their work. Thus the alchemist Gerard Dorn sees his own inner transformation reflected in the transformative processes of natural and organic growth, imagined as a metallic tree growing in the earth. He writes of 'the metallic tree growing in the midst of nature's womb; its trunk in the earth divided into different branches, spread throughout the whole globe of the earth, from Germany even as far as

Hungary and beyond; as in the human body veins are spread through different limbs, which are separated from one another'.

A mysterious fiery spirit liquid, variously identified with 'Philosophical Mercury' or *aqua permanens*, flows throughout the Philosophical Tree. And in one alchemical text, the *materia prima*, the mercurial liquid and the branching tree are united with the *lapis philosophorum* or Philosophical Stone, the most common symbol for both the source and goal of the process of transformation. 'The *prima materia* is an oily water, and is the philosophic stone from which branches multiply to infinity.'

In another text the student is advised: 'Plant this Tree upon the Stone, so that it fear not the buffetings of the wind.' Here, the Stone is both the potential seed, out of which will branch the tree of realization, and an image of the goal: the treasure, the 'jewel of great price' hidden in its roots.

Through his studies of alchemical symbolism Jung confirmed his view that it was for the purpose of strengthening the individual's conscious realization of the Self that the symbolic image of the Tree appeared in dreams and fantasies. For he had found that it most often appeared in dreams at critical periods in an individual's life, times when there was a pressing need for a supporting image of growth and integration. At times like these, this image answered the situation of the dreamer in a way that all the well-meaning advice in the world would have been unable to do.

In his *Alchemical Studies* Jung published a number of spontaneously imagined paintings of the Tree by people who knew nothing of alchemical or religious symbolism. Many of these were painted before Jung himself knew anything of the symbolic significance of the Tree image. It was only after studying comparative religion and mythology that he came to understand precisely why the unconscious so frequently produced this particular image. It was because the all-embracing image of the Cosmic Tree, standing at the centre with its roots and boughs uniting heaven and earth, was the most fitting symbol for the unconscious source (the root), the conscious realization (the trunk) and the 'trans-conscious' goal (the crown) of individuation, which upon the human plane is a continuation of the cosmic process itself. The unconscious could not choose a more fitting image to embody life's transformative processes and regenerative powers.

For the yogi and the mystic, who have overcome the guardians and gained mastery of the 'serpent power' that guards the Tree of Knowledge and Wisdom, the traditional images of Paradise become transparent symbols for the achieved state of interior ecstasy and bliss.

On the evening of the 27th day of the month of Rajab, the whole Muslim world celebrates the mystical ascent of the Prophet Mohammed. During this festival the mosques are specially lit, and services are held in which elaborate accounts of the Prophet's Night Journey (*lailatal-miraj*) are recited. These describe how Mohammed, in the company of the Archangel Gabriel and riding on the strange mythical beast Buraq, passes through the cosmic regions, descending into Hell and ascending into the seven Heavens to meet with the Prophets and the Blessed Ones in the gardens of Paradise (pls. 25, 26).

Islamic literature, following the example of the Koran, delights in describing these marvellous celestial gardens. Here the Blessed, clad in silken garments, are said to recline on bridal couches, served by dark-eyed houris and divine youths beneath trees of pure gold, glistening coral and mother of pearl, their branches laden with precious gems. At the centre of these fabulous gardens stands the Celestial Tree (pl. 24), the Tuba or Sidra, from which flow four rivers of purest water, milk, honey and wine; at their boundary stands the mysterious Lote Tree beyond which none may pass.

Mohammed's Night Journey was the exemplary model on which the mystics of Islam based their own ecstatic experiences. Thus, in the ninth century, the mystic Abu Bayid of Bistam wrote: '. . . my spirit was born to the heavens. It looked at nothing and gave no heed, though Paradise and Hell were displayed to it, for it was freed of phenomena and veils. Then I became as a bird, whose body was of Oneness and whose wings were of Everlastingness, and I continued to fly in the air of the Absolute, until I passed into the sphere of purification, and gazed upon the field of Eternity, and beheld the Tree of Oneness.'

In the fourteenth century, Persia's greatest lyric poet, the mystic Hafiz, wrote in similar vein:

> On the holy boughs of the Sidra,
> High up in the heavenly fields,
> Beyond terrestrial desire,
> My soul-bird a warm nest has built.

It is not only in literature that this Islamic 'nostalgia for Paradise' is expressed; all the arts of Islam are pervaded by it. For they all seek, by means of images which reflect the other worldly beauty of the celestial realms, to awaken in fallen and forgetful man a deep and burning longing for the paradisal state: that one *ultimately real* mode of being for which the soul thirsts.

In the West, Islamic art is most widely known for its carpets, and these carpets offer us a marvellous lesson in what Bachelard calls 'concrete metaphysics'. For they all, more or less explicitly, imitate the form and layout of the celestial gardens of the Islamic paradise. At the call to prayer, which interrupts profane activities throughout the Muslim world four times a day, the Muslim in the market place unrolls his prayer carpet in the direction of Mecca, the sacred centre of the Islamic cosmos and the place where Mohammed's celestial ascent began. The carpet on which the Muslim kneels in prayer is a heavenly field – a sacred space separate from the profane and worldly space of his everyday activities. Within this sacred space he ascends on the rhythm of his prayer to that paradisal plane where the Blessed Ones, who have achieved that mode of being for which his soul thirsts, eternally abide. This symbolism is expressed in the actual fabric of the Islamic carpet, the patterning of which so often combines the centred Tree or Herb of Life with the motives of expansion, ascent and flight (pl. 30).

The Tree of History

The archetypal image of the Tree was central to the revolutionary thought of one philosopher whose vision of history was to influence the whole course of Western thought.

Joachim of Floris (1135–1202) was a contemplative mystic whose whole thought was moulded by a series of intense inner visions and illuminations. The most important of these occurred one Pentecost, while he was studying the Book of Revelation, in which St John describes his vision of the Tree of Life. It was Joachim's own vision of this tree that became the generative image for his dynamic vision of history (pl. 42).

The prevailing attitude to history in Joachim's time was the static one of St Augustine, who said that the thousand-year reign of Christ, prophesied in Revelation, was embodied here and now in the teachings of the Church under whose law and protection all would remain until the Last Judgment. Joachim, who was not consciously unorthodox or subversive, and who worked with the approval of no less than three popes, developed a totally new and dynamic view of history. Aided by his vision of the tree, Joachim saw history as an unfolding process, ascending in three stages, each identified with one of the Three Persons of the Trinity. The first was the Age of the Father, when men were subject to the Tables of the Law, as given to Moses on Mount Sinai by Yahweh, the Old Testament God. The second was the Age of the Son, when instead of Fear, Faith predominated, and when the word of God was given to men through the Gospel and the Sacraments administered by the Church. The third was the Age of the Holy Spirit, when love would preside, and when the Dove of the Holy Spirit would descend directly into men's hearts and they would receive immediate revelations from God unmediated by either Law or Church. What was really new was Joachim's idea of the overlapping of these periods. For just as each new shoot on the tree grows out of the one preceding it, so the periods of history overlap, each stage germinating the one which is to come. According to Joachim, the gestation of the first period lasted from Adam until the time of Abraham; that of the second from Elijah to the time of Christ; and that of the third from the time of St Benedict, who founded the monasteries, to around the time when Joachim himself was working. Later his followers fixed the beginning of the third period proper, the Age of the Holy Spirit, in the year 1260. Curiously enough, it is around this time that some modern historians see the beginnings of the 'modern period'. The fact that they do so is a reflection of their debt to Joachim himself, who was the first to conceive of the historical process as a continuum in which the fruits of the past contain the seeds of the future. For Joachim's idea of the third dispensation of the Holy Spirit implies the unprecedented idea of the fallibility of the Church and the inevitable dissolution of its mediating power.

This idea caught on and led to the millennial movements of the Middle Ages, when the discontent of the masses, congregating for the first time around great cities, sought salvation in the immediate realization of the Third Age. The Antichrist Pope would be finally overthrown, perfect peace and love would descend, and the Kingdom of God on earth would be realized. All this hastened the coming of the Reformation, through which Joachim's ideas passed into the mainstream of Western philosophy, where they were taken up by the German idealist philosophers Lessing, Schelling and Fichte, and by Auguste Comte, with his idea of the three phases of history: the theological, the metaphysical and the scientific. Finally, they formed the background to the Third Reich (or Thousand-Year Reich) of National Socialism; to the Marxist idea of the three stages, of primitive communism, class society and the final classless communism of the future; and to what is often called the 'radical secularization' of modern times, along with its dangerous doctrine of infinite progress.

All this shows the tremendous power for creative and destructive transformation that an archetypal image can have. Joachim would, of course, have been horrified at these later developments, and particularly at the distorted use to which his ideas had been put. Had he known of them he might well have quoted these words from St Paul, which appear no less than thirty-six times in his two main works, the *Liber concordiae* and *Expositio*: 'The Letter killeth but the Spirit giveth Light' (II Corinthians 3:6). For it was the literal application of the letter of Joachim's ideas which so distorted them that his revelation of the inner meaning of historical events was largely ignored.

The Tree of Inner Necessity

A visionary who did discern the inner meaning of Joachim's ideas, most especially his idea of the 'third' revelation, was the great pioneer of non-representational painting, Wassily Kandinsky. In his autobiographical essay *Reminiscences* (1913) he used Joachim's Trinitarian tree-image to illustrate his own vision of the spiritual evolution of art:

'Today is one of the great revelations of this world. Here begins the great epoch of the spiritual, the revelation of the Spirit – Father, Son and Holy Spirit.

'Art is like religion in many respects. Its development does not consist of new discoveries which strike out old truths. . . . Its development consists of . . . new truths which are basically nothing more than the organic development, the organic growing, of earlier wisdom which is not voided by the later, but as wisdom and truth continues to live and produce. The trunk of the tree does not become superfluous because of a new branch; it makes the branch possible. Would the New Testament have been possible without the Old? Would our epoch of the threshold of the "third" revelation be conceivable without the second?'

And what, according to Kandinsky, are the 'necessary elements for the reception of the "third" revelation, the revelation of the Holy Spirit'? There is but one, 'a single demand: the demand of *inner life*', or, as he often puts it in his writings, the demand of *inner necessity*.

It was on the basis of inner necessity, as exemplified in plant growth, that both Kandinsky and his friend and fellow-teacher, Paul Klee, founded their famous 'point-line to plane' theories of form production. Thus, Klee told his students at the Bauhaus of 'the irritated point as latent energy':

'At the slightest impetus, the point is about to emerge from a state in which its mobility is concealed, to move onwards, to take on one or more directions. It is about to become linear. In concrete pictorial terms: the seed strikes root. Initially the line is directed earthwards, though not to dwell there, only to draw energy thence for reaching up into the air.

'The point of origin between soil and atmosphere stretches out, and the generalized plant image becomes tree, root, trunk, crown. The trunk is the medium for the rising of the sap from the soil to the lofty crown. The linear forces gather within it to form a powerful stream, and they radiate outwards, in order to pervade the airspace at free height. Hence forward articulation naturally becomes more and more ramified and open, to make the best of air and light. Leaves become flat lobes, the whole thing begins to resemble a lung, or gills, porous, subdivided, for a single purpose. Let this entire organism now become an example to us – a structure functioning from within to without or vice versa. Let us learn: The whole form results from a single base, the base of inner necessity. Need is at the bottom.'

On the occasion of an exhibition of his works at Jena in 1924, Klee gave the famous lecture which was published under the title *On Modern Art*. In it he used the parable of the Tree to describe the creative process at work within the artist. The modern artist does not wilfully distort or deform his experience of nature, life and art, but, like the trunk of the tree, naturally transforms it, for 'no one will expect a tree to form its crown in exactly the same way as its roots'. All the artist does 'in his appointed place in the tree trunk, is to gather what rises from the depths and pass it on. He neither serves nor commands, but only acts as a go-between. His position is humble. He himself is not the beauty of the crown; it has merely passed through him.'

Throughout his writings, and in his teaching, Klee continually drew parallels between natural and organic processes and the creative process. For he saw human creativity as a continuation of the cosmic process. In itself, this idea can be used as an illustration of Klee's parable of the crown and the roots. For he himself drew it out of the past, inheriting it from the German Romantics, and then transforming it through the 'trunk' of his own personal practice into the 'crown' of his work as a thinker and an artist.

Goethe, with whom Klee had such an affinity, was possessed throughout his life by images of organic growth and their relationship to the poetic process. As a young man he had searched passionately for what he called the *Urpflanze*, the primordial plant, which was not so much a botanical species as the projection of the dynamic pattern underlying all natural growth. Goethe's intermingling of aesthetic feeling and biological speculation was also exemplified in the work of his close friend Carl Gustav Carus (1789–1864). Carus, besides being a comparative anatomist and speculative psychologist, was a well-known landscape painter: he is particularly important since he was one of the precursors of the theory of the unconscious which has played so great a part in the cultural transformation of our own time, and without which the poetic universe of a painter like Klee would be unthinkable (pl. 58). In his treatise *Nature and Idea*, he pictured man's mental life as a plant, rooted in the soil of the unconscious and growing upwards towards the 'divine light' of greater consciousness (see p. 111).

This fundamental identity between man's inner psychic life and vegetal life was the basic assumption underlying the Romantic poets' and painters' emphasis on creative imagination. Thus the organic view of imagination was used to counter the eighteenth century's mechanistic model of man's inner workings. The distinction was continually drawn between the conscious, artificial and mechanical piecing together of a work of art from known models and the organic fusing of disparate parts into a whole by the naturally eruptive and cohesive force of imagination. Thus the poet Edward Young had written, as early as 1759: 'An *Original* may be said to be of a *vegetable* nature; it rises spontaneously from the vital root of genius; it *grows*, it is not *made*.'

Coleridge, paraphrasing the German philosopher Schlegel, wrote: 'The form is mechanic when on any given material we impress a pre-determined form. The organic form, on the other hand, is innate; it shapes as it develops itself from within.... Nature, the prime genial artist, inexhaustible in diverse powers, is equally inexhaustible in forms. Each exterior is the physiognomy of the being within.'

Another quotation from Coleridge's writings aptly characterizes the inner thrust of the whole Romantic movement, as well as its continued repercussions in twentieth-century art; inviting the individual to participate actively in the regenerative processes embodied in the Tree, Coleridge writes: 'What a plant is by an act not its own and unconsciously, that thou must *make* thyself to become.'

1 The Tree as a symbol of the psyche. The psychologist C. G. Jung described the dream-image of the tree as a symbol of the 'self depicted as a process of growth' and saw it as exemplifying what he called the process of individuation. Jung's findings are prefigured in this diagram by the eighteenth-century English mystic William Law. A beam of light from the world of consciousness pierces the 'dark world' of the unconscious in which the tree of man's spiritual and psychological development is rooted. Passing through the 'fire world' of suffering and experience, it opens out in the light of greater consciousness towards the light of God. (The Tree of the Soul, figure by William Law from *The Works of Jacob Behmen* [*Boehme*], London, 1764–81.)

2, 3, 4 In the ancient and archaic world the tree is not worshipped for itself only, but because it reveals the workings of a 'wholly other' power or sacred force, which man both fears and venerates. This power manifests itself at the cosmic centre and radiates throughout the whole. As a living embodiment of both the centre and the whole, the sacred tree becomes the Cosmic Tree, which by its natural laws of development (its annual 'death' and 'rebirth') embodies the perpetual regeneration of the Cosmos from the Source. (2 Bulls flanking the Tree of Life, bronze bowl, Assyro-Kassite period, 13th-10th c. BC; 3 Gilgamesh and Enkidu the bull-man, wrestling with the sacred bull, seal impression, Assyrian, 2nd millennium BC; 4 King Ashurnasirpal II and a winged god worshipping the sacred tree, alabaster relief from Nimrud, Neo-Assyrian, 9th c. BC.)

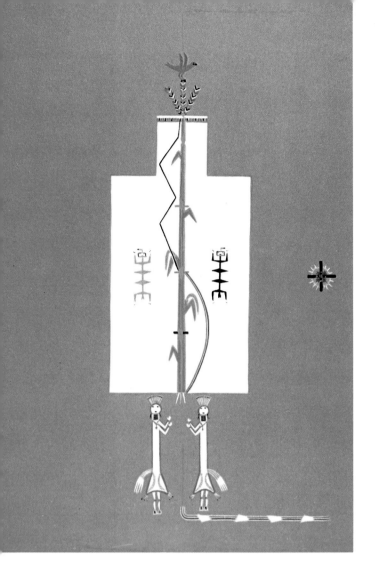

5 Up the giant corn plant, between female spirit guardians, goes the 'pollen-path' or 'blessing-way' of the Navaho Indians of the American Southwest. On one side of the plant, the masculine zig-zag of lightning; on the other, the feminine curve of the rainbow; above, the bird of happiness, signifying ultimate freedom, transcendence, flight. (Tree of Life, Navaho sandpainting, New Mexico.)

6 The tragic ambiguities and polarities of existence in time and space open out from the centre. Birth, Life, Death and Regeneration are embodied in these trees of the cardinal directions. At the top (east), the tree of the rising sun standing between the god of that name and the god of sharp-cutting-stone. To the right, the tree of sacrifice, between the maize god and the lord of the dead. At the foot of the picture, a tree surmounted by a humming-bird between the goddess of flowers and the goddess of drunkenness. Finally, split in the middle like a vulva, the tree of regeneration between the god of rain and the god of the underworld. (The five regions of the world, from Mayer Fejérváry Codex, Mixtec, Mexico, before AD 1350.)

7, 8 The tree as the axis of the universe. The Buddhist stupa, represented
here by a Japanese temple pagoda and a miniature Indian stupa, is an
image of the sacred centre of the world, that still point from which all
creation emanates. The cosmic axis or Axis Mundi, the linear extension
of this cosmogonic point, passes through the various planes of being
(shown here by the flat discs, the circles and squares of heaven and earth)
that constitute the multiple levels of the cosmos. It was here at the centre,

beneath the Cosmic Tree, that Prince Siddhartha, the future Buddha, attained enlightenment. At one with the Axis Mundi which ensures communication between these planes, the Buddha could transcend the human condition at will, and enter into intimate and compassionate communion with all beings at all levels. (7 Buddhist shrine in the form of a miniature stupa, Swat Valley, Pakistan; 8 Horyu-ji pagoda, Nara, Japan, *c.* AD 670–714.)

9 In his autobiography, Black Elk, the holy man of the Oglala Sioux, tells of the 'great vision' that he had when he was nine years old, in which he was carried off to the centre of the world where he met the 'Grandfathers', the 'Powers of the World' – 'them that have awakened all the beings of the earth with roots, legs and wings' – who appeared to him both as old men 'old like hills, like stars' and as the horses of the four quarters. From them he receives a bow ('the power to destroy'), a herb ('day-break-star herb, herb of power and understanding'), a pipe of peace, and a branch from the Tree of Life: 'a flowering stick . . . that was alive . . . and sprouted from the top and sent forth branches, and on the branches many leaves came out and murmured, and in the leaves the birds began to sing. "It shall stand in the centre of the nation's circle," said the Grandfather, "a cane to walk with and a people's heart; and by your powers you shall make it blossom."' (Black Elk at the centre of the world, watercolour by Standing Bear, Dakota, 20th c.)

10 The roots of the tree spread down far and wide into the hidden and mysterious depths of the earth, from where they draw up the vital sap of life, which, ascending through the trunk to the crown of the Cosmic Tree, becomes the heavenly elixir of immortality. In Egypt the Tree of Life from which the dead received eternal life was the sycamore fig. Here, the goddess of the tree, epiphany of the Great Earth Mother from whom all things derive their sustenance, pours down the precious 'water of the depths'. (The Goddess of the sycamore fig welcoming the deceased, wall-painting, tomb of Panehsy, Thebes, 16th–14th c. BC.)

11 Throughout Africa and in many other parts of the world, sap-filled trees have been regarded as the embodiment of divine motherhood. The sycamore fig, which like most figs exudes a milky sap, was associated with Isis and the other Egyptian mother goddesses, Nut the goddess of heaven, and Hathor, the cow goddess. All are epiphanies of the Great Mother. (Thoutmosis III suckled by Isis in the guise of a sycamore tree, wall-painting, tomb of Thoutmosis III, Thebes, 16th–14th c. BC.)

12 As well as embodying divine motherhood, the tree can also embody the male potency needed to fecundate the womb of the Great Earth Mother. Here Isis worships the tree-pillar of Osiris, the dying and resurrected god of vegetation (see p. 14). In her right hand she holds the *crux ananta* or ankh – the Egyptian looped cross, hieroglyph for life and happiness. Later the Coptic Church of Egypt associated this sign with the dying and resurrected god of Christianity. (Sacrifice to the Osiris pillar, stone relief, temple of Rameses I, Abydos, *c.* 1315–1292 BC.)

13 Queen Maya, the mother of Buddha, in the traditional posture of a fertility goddess. She stands upon a centre of divine manifestation, an open lotus flower, and clasps a branch of the sacred sal tree, the tree under which the Buddha was born. (Maya with a branch of the Asoka Tree, gilt bronze and stones, Nepal, 18th c.)

14 According to the elaborate classifications of the Indian love poets of the sixteenth and seventeenth centuries, love is of two kinds: love in union and love in separation. Love in separation has three stages according to the intensity of desire or anxiety felt by the beloved: (1) longing for union; (2) anxiety which continues to rack the body till a meeting is effected; (3) sickness, when the fever of love increases and the body wastes away. Here the first is represented. Alone on the terrace of the palace, the beloved pines for her departed lover. Clasping the trunk of the tree, she longs for the joys of love in union. (Woman embracing a tree, miniature, Guler, Punjab Hills, early 19th c.)

15, 16 A tree need lose none of its concrete natural qualities when it becomes symbolic and embodies the Tree of Life. For it is through these natural qualities which manifest the laws of organic development (such as seasonal change) that the tree is experienced as a microcosm, embodying the power of the sacred which, from a single centre, radiates throughout the cosmos. Here (left) an offering is placed on the bole of a tree which manifests this force. At another level of culture, the tree which manifests the sacred becomes an elaborated and formalized religious symbol with a complex and exemplary iconography, as in this Javanese temple carving (right) of a Buddhist wishing-tree. (15 Votive mask in a tree, India; 16 Buddhist wishing-tree, relief from Lara-Djanggrang, Java, 9th c. A D.)

17 The birth of the Greek god of vegetation, Adonis, from the trunk of a myrrh tree which miraculously burst after a ten-month gestation. (Birth of Adonis, bowl, Urbino, 16th c.)

18 Clasping the branch of a sacred sal tree in the manner of an Indian fertility goddess, Queen Maya miraculously gives birth to the future Buddha from her right side. Equally miraculous was the Buddha's conception. Queen Maya dreamt that a white elephant descended from heaven (top right) and entered her right side (lower right). As soon as he is born the Buddha takes up a position at the 'centre of the world'. Stepping upon lotuses, he takes seven strides and makes the 'difficult ascent' (*Durohana*), ascending symbolically through the seven planetary heavens to the summit of the world. Here, as one Buddhist text recalls, 'He looks at the regions all around and says with a voice like that of a bull: "I am at the top of the world; this is my last birth; for me there will never be another existence."' (Birth of Buddha, painting, Tibet.)

19 Fourteen branches tipped with birds and buds open out from a central stem, on which is the lotus-sun-wheel surmounted by a serpent, its tail coiled in two loops and its hood extended. Two monkey-headed figures cling to the stem, whose base is flanked by two bulls. All life is created and sustained from the centre. (Tree of Life and Knowledge, bronze, India, Vigayanagar period, 1336–1546.)

20 Standing under the Kadamba Tree sacred to him, upon the lotus throne, centre of divine manifestation, at the centre of the world, the Hindu god Krishna sustains the life of the universe by the power of his music, drawing the hearts of all beings towards the centre, where the sacred manifests itself. (Krishna fluting, miniature, Jodhpur, early 19th c.)

21 In the Javanese shadow theatre (*wayang*), this object, called a *gunungan* ('mountain') or *kekayon* ('tree'), represents the sacred centre around which the play of divine and demonic forces develops. The winged doors, a motif found in Javanese architecture (see p. 118), suggest both a 'passing-through' and a 'magical flight' from this world to the supernatural world in which the mythical drama takes place. (*Gunungan*, leather, Java, 18th c.)

22 This Assembly Tree of the Gods (Ts'ogs-shing) shows Tsongkapa, one of the greatest Bodhisattvas of Tibet, at the cosmic centre with the image of Buddha in front of his chest. Surrounding him on all sides are the whole assembly of teachers, Buddhas, Bodhisattvas, female deities, guardians of the faith and gods of the four directions. The trunk of the tree arises from the primordial waters, from which all things arise, and to which they will all return. (Assembly Tree of the Gods, *tanka*, Tibet, early 19th c.?)

23, 24 Modern depth psychology has established that every man unconsciously longs to realize himself, to actualize his potentiality for wholeness and freedom. He is goaded on in this endeavour by unconscious projections of that wholeness; images and symbols that are ciphers for the unity and plentitude of being. This innate longing is reflected in the nostalgia for Paradise which is present in one form or other at all levels of culture. It is evoked here in two images from the arts of Islam: on the right, a celestial tree-house in the gardens of Paradise, and on the left, the centre of a Persian 'garden carpet', which represents the heavenly gardens with the four rivers of Paradise radiating from their centre. (23 Garden carpet, Persian, 17th–18th c.; 24 Garden of the Angels, coloured and gilt drawing, Persia, Fabriz school, mid-16th c.)

25, 26 These two pictures represent Mohammed's Night Journey, during which the prophet of Islam travelled along the Axis Mundi, descending into the depths of hell and ascending from Mecca, the sacred centre of the Islamic world, through Jerusalem and the seven planetary spheres that make up the heavenly world. The various accounts of this event differ in many respects; sometimes the ascent is made by means of a ladder, sometimes by means of a tree (both symbols of the Axis Mundi), and sometimes it is simply stated that the Prophet was 'taken up'. Here

Mohammed rides upon the strange mythical beast, Buraq. In the picture on the left, the Archangel Gabriel shows Mohammed (not shown) the Tree of Ez-Zakkoum, the Infernal Thorn Tree that was planted for the torment of the wicked. In the right-hand picture the Prophet is shown a tree of rubies, sapphires and emeralds, perhaps the miraculous Tuba Tree which stood at the centre of the Islamic Paradise. Mohammed's Night Journey became the model on which mystics based descriptions of their experiences (see p. 28). (Miniatures by Mi'raj-nameh, Turkey, 15th c.)

27, 28 The Cosmic Tree not only embodies the unity and diversity of the cosmos but also expresses both ascent and expansion. In the poet Rilke's words:

> *It develops its being in roundness*
> *Slowly giving itself*
> *The form that eliminates*
> *Hazards of wind.*

In the left-hand picture we see the worship of the Tree of Enlightenment (Bodhi) under which the Buddha sat. Image of the endless regeneration of the cosmos from a single transcendent source, it is represented here as growing from a single seed (*bija*), which was the name given to the relic around which the Buddhist stupas at Sanchi were built. Below, a Chinese Cosmic Tree, the trunk of which curves in on itself, as though gathering force and concentration for its ascension and expansion into space. (27 The Bodhi Tree, relief from the Great Stupa, Sanchi, India, 1st c. A D; 28 Tree of the Universe, rubbing of relief from Chamber of the Offerings, by Won Yong, China, A D 168.)

29 Two horsemen meeting at a tree, symbol of the centre; a common design on bowls of this type. (Rayy mina'i ware bowl, Persia, early 13th c.)

30 At the call of prayer, which interrupts profane activities throughout the Muslim world four times a day, the Muslim in the market-place would unroll his prayer carpet in the direction of Mecca, the sacred centre of the Islamic world, and the place where Mohammed began his celestial ascent. The carpet upon which he kneels is a sacred space, qualitatively different from the profane space of his everyday world. The patterning of Islamic carpets express this difference, for they all more or less explicitly imitate the form and layout of the celestial gardens of Paradise (see pl. 23), and, like this one, combine the centred image of the Tree or Herb of Life with motifs of expansion, ascent and flight. (Soumak carpet, Caucasus, 18th c.)

31 In this Renaissance drawing of the legend of Theseus and the Minotaur the artist unconsciously makes reference to the Tree as cosmic centre. According to the Greek philosophers Parmenides and Plato, being itself is round. Here, Theseus holds up the 'sphere of being' (the ball of thread given him by Ariadne), which along with the Labyrinth and the Tree exemplifies the life-process, the existential unfolding of

man's essential being in time and space. In the background Ariadne stands stranded on the island of Naxos, where Theseus left her, whilst his father, Aegeus, seeing the black sails of the ship and believing Theseus to be dead, throws himself into the sea. (Theseus and the Labyrinth, drawing from *Florentine Picture Chronicle*, Italy, *c.* 1460–70.)

بر فراز درخت طاقی نهشت   با ره وبه کی روان از و بگشت   کرد پریواز از از فراز درخت

32 As centred images exemplifying the unfolding of man's potentiality for wholeness, miraculous trees frequently occur in myths and legends. The Persian mystic Asafi describes the mystic's quest for wholeness as an allegory of love: 'Everyone who has some knowledge of the heart may contemplate my serious words, because this story of Jamal and Jalal is entirely due to the mystery of ecstasy.' Jalal, whose name means Glory, sets out to win Jamal, daughter of Mihrarai, the king of the angelic beings who live at the summit of Mount Qaf. During Jalal's quest, Jamal, whose name means Beauty, appears to him fleetingly as different birds, turtledove, peahen, and parrot, in the branches of trees on the way. As he journeys he passes through fabulous gardens where 'flowers speak like parrots and sing like nightingales', and at one point he comes to a miraculous tree upon whose leaves the name of Jamal is written. (Jalal before the mystical tree, miniature, Persia, late 15th c.)

33 In the course of his conquests, Alexander the Great comes upon a talking tree, which rebukes him for his ambition and prophesies his death in a country far from his native land. (Alexander and the talking tree, miniature from the *Shah Namah*, Persia, 15th c.)

34–36 The great Indian Emperor Akbar (1542–1605) was obsessed with the underlying unity of religions. The tree-pillar (symbol of unity) in the central picture is the one on which he sat to lead discussions between representatives of the world religions. On either side are shown other tree-pillars, whose regenerative curves and serpentine rhythms emphasize the mysterious process of transformation, the rising of the sap. (34 Buddhist pillar with the lotus form and the Tree of Enlightenment, relief, Amaravati, India, 2nd c. AD; 35 Akbar's column in the Diwan-i-Khas, Fatehpur Sikri, 16th c.; 36 Columns of the doorway of Saint-Lazare, Avallon, France, end 11th c.)

37 *overleaf* As well as symbolizing the union or 'marriage' of opposites, the tree can also symbolize their tragic split, as in this medieval manuscript of the Tree of Good and Evil as a twofold Tree of Vices and Virtues. On either page the Vices and Virtues are exactly paired, the twelve virtues growing from *Caritas* (Charity), the mother of all the virtues, and the twelve vices from *Cupiditas* (Greed), the mother of all vices. The *Arbor bona* is associated with the Church (*Ecclesia fidelium*), and each of the virtues is represented by a female figure in a medallion and by the foliage of some 'noble' shrub or tree; pine, terebinth, rose, box, cedar and the like. On the other hand, the *Arbor mala*, associated with the Synagogue, is represented by a single species, the withered fig tree of the Gospel, on which no fruit grows (Matthew 21:19), and to whose roots the 'axe is laid' (Matthew 3:10). (Tree of Good and Evil, miniature from Lambert of Saint-Omer, *Liber floridus*, before 1192.)

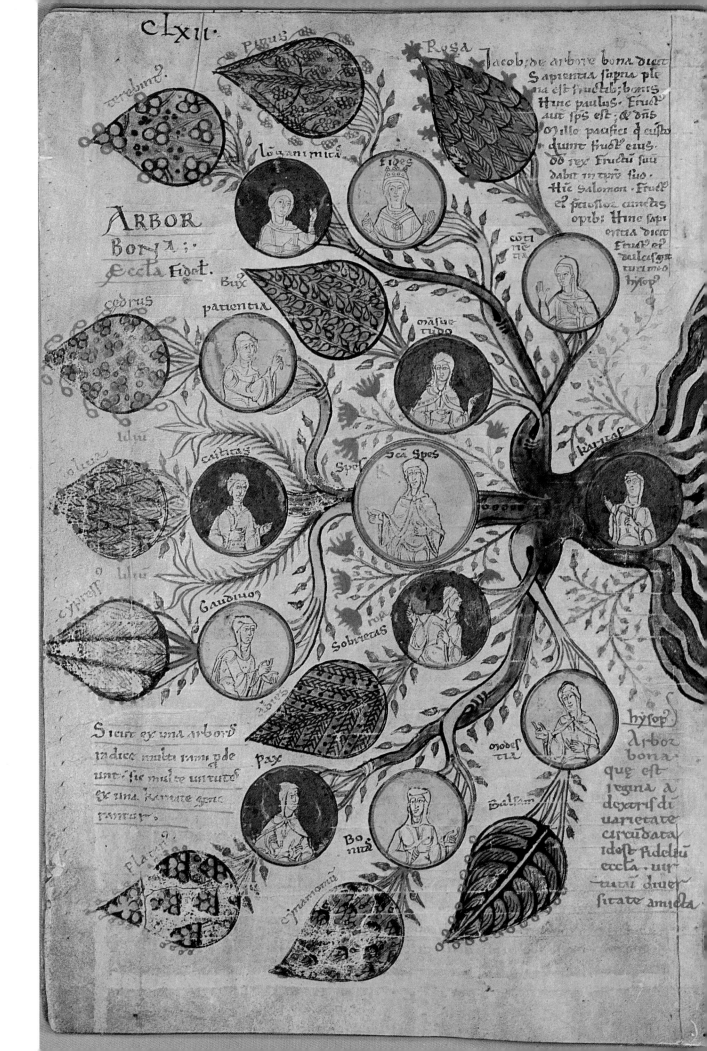

ARBOR
BONA;·
ECCLA FIDET.

Iacob; de arbore bona dicit
Sapientia sapia ple-
na est fructib; bonis
Hinc paulus· Fruct
aut ips est; & dns
op illo pacifer q custo
diunt fruct eius·
od rex Fructu suu
dabit in tpre suo·
Hic Salomon· Fruct
et pastor cunctas
opib; Hinc sapi-
entia dicit
Fruct ei
dulcis sp
tuelmeo
hysop

terebint.   Pinus   Rosa

loganimitas   Fides

Bux   continentia

cedrus   patientia   masuetudo

castitas   Sca Spes   karitas

cypress   Gaudium   Sobrietas   modestia

Sicut ex una arbore
radice multi rami pde
unt: sic multe uirtutes
ex una karitate gene
rantur·

pax   Bo   Balsam   hysop
        nita   Arbor
                          bona
                          que est
                          regina a
                          dexris di
                          uarietate
                          circudata
                          idest fideliu
                          eccla· uir
                          tutum diuer
                          sitate amicta

Platan
cinamomu

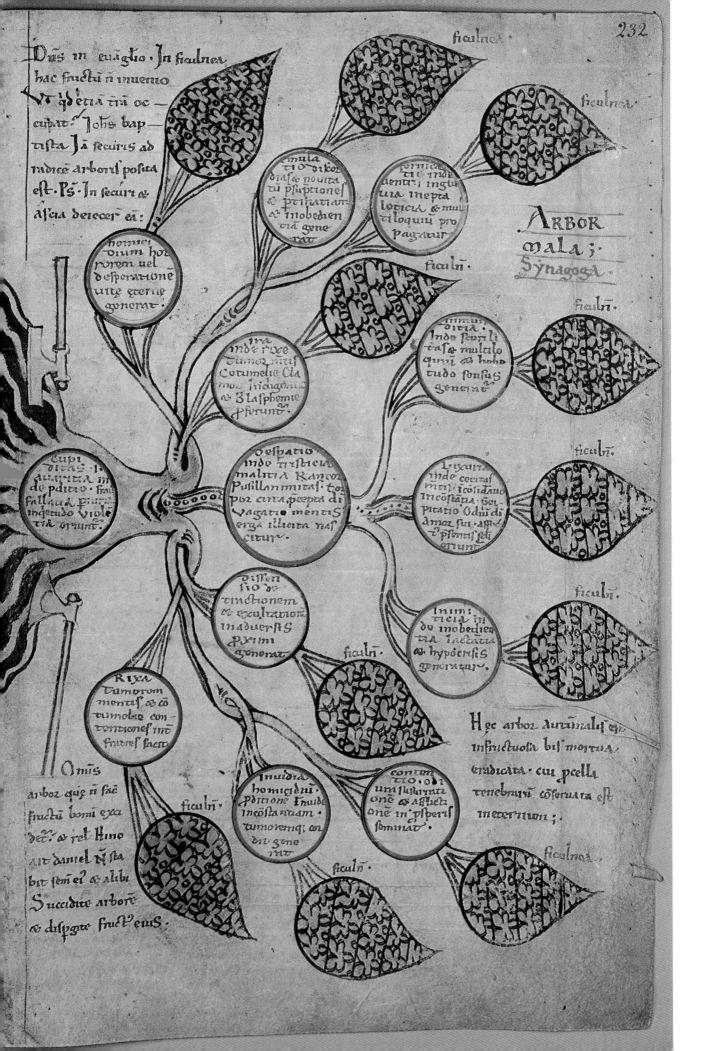

ARBOR
mala;
Synagoga.

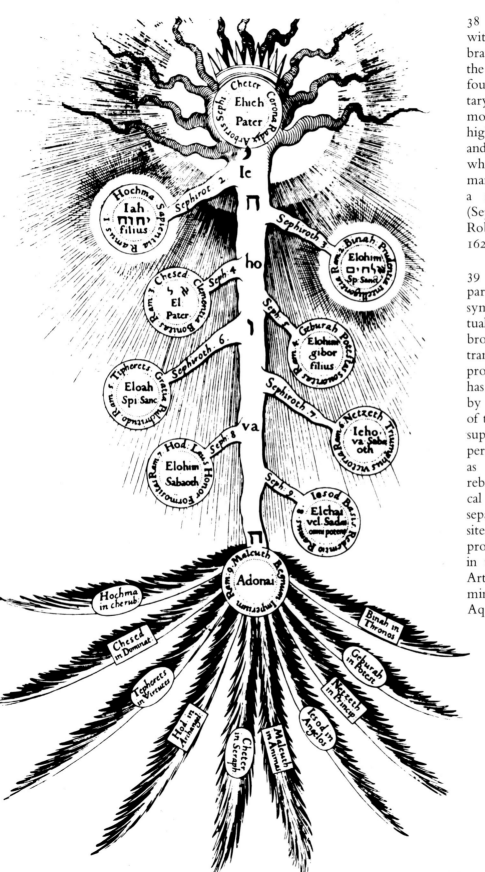

38 The inverted tree, the tree with its roots in heaven and its branches growing down towards the earth, is a primary image found both at the most elementary levels of culture and at the most complex. It has been most highly elaborated in the Indian and Judaic mystical traditions where it is a symbol for the manifestation of the cosmos from a single transcendent source. (Sephirotic Tree, engraving from Robert Fludd, *Philosophia sacra*, 1626.)

39 It was by means of his total participation in the images and symbols that mirrored his spiritual condition that the alchemist brought about his own inner transformation. The alchemical process reflects what C. G. Jung has called individuation, whereby an individual becomes aware of the unconscious (neglected or suppressed) sides of his total personality. This is experienced as an initiation, a death and rebirth, pictured in this alchemical manuscript as a dissolution, separation and synthesis of opposites into a new unity. The whole process and its goal are embodied in the image of the tree. (The Artist and the Mystic Sister, miniature from St Thomas Aquinas(?), *De alchimia*, 16th c.)

Er manto corpora metallia sisti
tantur per spiritum proprium su

miges ponum entendre. ceus ki sunt li seint hume. ke il ne put point de hume sere escumegez choses deuaunt gent.
Homicides il apeler ceus ki tuwent houmes. e ceus ki portent haine en lur quœrs. Mutes maneres sut de fornicatiun
En tutes les maneres ke houme fet le desir de lur char sauns sa femme espuse: ceo est apele fornicatiun. E il i ad forni
catiu de pensee. Venimauns sut ceus ki tuwent la gent p uenim. e ceus ki sement descord entre freres. Idolatres sunt ceu
ki aurent ydles. e les autres ausi. Mensunges sut akcuns ki sunt nunbres entre legers peccches. Nus mentum sument p
qdaunce. e peruersure. ene mi p malice. il ne dist pas de teus mensunges. Autres mensunges sut ki sut morteaus. Si tu
mesunge. de desleaute. e de blasfemie. e ki uenent de haine. e de enuie. e de auarice. e deueine glore. E sachez ke se
ur iohan dist. deus est uerite. e nule re ne est si cuntrarie a uerite cu mensunge. Bunt la prie des mentirs serra en lee
taunk de fu e de sufre. Bunt la misericorde de deu nus garde p sa prie. ki uit en regne en secle de secles amen.

40 At the end of time, the Tree of Life stands at the centre of the Heavenly City, Jerusalem. 'And [the angel] shewed me a pure river of water of life, clear as crystal, proceeding out of the throne of God and of the Lamb. In the midst of the street of it, and on either side of the river, was . . . the tree of life, which bare twelve manner of fruits, and yielded her fruits every month; and the leaves of the tree were for the healing of the nations.' (Revelation 22:1–2). (Heavenly Jerusalem, miniature from Apocalypse, 13th c.)

41 The commentary on the Apocalypse of St John by Beatus (d.789), abbot of San Martín de Liebana in northern Spain, enjoyed great popularity throughout Spain and beyond for some five centuries. Quite often to be found in the manuscripts are representations of the just man climbing a palm tree, which illustrate the Psalm verses: 'The righteous shall flourish like the palm tree: he shall grow like a cedar in Lebanon.' (Psalm 92:12.) (Miniature from Beatus, *Commentarius in Apocalypsin*, AD 975.)

42 The Tree of History, one of the *figurae* of the Trinitarian Tree used by the medieval visionary Joachim of Floris to expound his theory of the three *status*, stages or states of history. Out of Noah, who represents the age or state of the Father, grow two stems representing his two sons Shem and Japhet, from whom sprang the two great peoples of the world, the Gentiles and the Jews. These stems cross just above the head of Christ, who represents the age or state of the Son. They then continue their separate paths until they cross once more above the Dove of the Holy Spirit, which symbolizes the third age or state, when, as can be seen from the joined branches in the centre of the circle, the Jews and Gentiles will be reconciled. (Miniature from Joachim of Floris, *Liber figurarum*, 13th c.)

43 Here the tree is used to expound the history of man's life, the 'like or unlike or various conditions of all men in their estate of Creation, birth, life, death, buriall, resurrection, and last Judgement with pyous observations out of the Scriptures upon the severall branches'. (The Tree of Man's Life, engraving by John Goddard, from broadsheet, 1649.)

THE TREE OF MANS LIFE

Or an Emblem declareing the like, and vnlike, or various condition of all men in their estate of Creation,
birth, life, death, buriall, resurrection, and last Iudgment. with pyous obseruations out of
the Scriptures vpon the seuerall branches.

To the right worshipfull and virtueous Lady the Lady Susanna Vernatti; R: D: wisheth encrease of the best blessings in this life, and fruition of eternall ioy and felicitie
in the life to come, humbly dedicating his endeauours, and desireing fauourable acceptance of his best seruices.

CHRIST

By Ri: Dey
Batch: in arts

Yohn Goddard sculpsit

A Wee are all borne alike, and equall being in our infancie contented with milke.
B Wee liue vnlike, and after milke not satisfyed with whole kingdomes, and now a dayer
   there is no end of riches, and pleagures.
C Wee dye alike, the royall scepter haueing not more prerogatiues then the cripples crutch.

D Though wee be buryed vnlike, and couered with purple, or cheaper cloth, yet wee are all alike wormes meate.
E Wee shall arise alike, at the last day: spite of all the dying vanities of fortune.
F Wee shall be rewarded vnlike, either from Lazarus, or the rich glutons table with blessed or
   cursed estate for euer.

44, 45 In Blake's painting (right) it is Christ himself who leads Adam and Eve out of the Garden of Innocence into the World of Experience where what was potential must be fulfilled. The Tree of Life and the Tree of Knowledge of Good and Evil can be seen to represent the two temptations between which man perpetually stands (p. 24). In the medieval miniature (above) the two trees are pictured as one, the tree on which grow the fruits of Life and Death which condition human existence. (44 Tree of Death and Life, miniature by Berthold Furtmeyer, from Archbishop of Salzburg's missal, 1481; 45 Fall of Man, watercolour by William Blake, 1807.)

46 The Great Cross of the Lateran in Rome, an early Christian mosaic showing the Cross at the centre of the world with the four rivers of Paradise, and the Tree of Life (surmounted by the Phoenix, symbol of Christ) in the midst of the Heavenly City, guarded by the Archangel Michael. (Christ above Jerusalem, mosaic in San Giovanni in Laterano, Rome, as last restored by Torini, 1884.)

47 This mosaic most likely played an important part in the dissemination in Europe of the ancient Near Eastern iconographic motif of the Tree of Life and confronted animals (pls. 2, 3); for it was made by Saracen craftsmen as part of the Arabo-Norman palace of the Christian King Roger II of Sicily at Palermo, where many of the most beautiful and costly Byzantine textiles (which often incorporate this motif) were made. Confronting the date-palm at the top is Sagittarius, the archer-centaur, half animal, half man; like the Tree, he is a symbol for the union of Heaven and Earth; he aims at the centre. (Mosaic, Stanze del Palazzo, Palermo, Norman, 1160–70.)

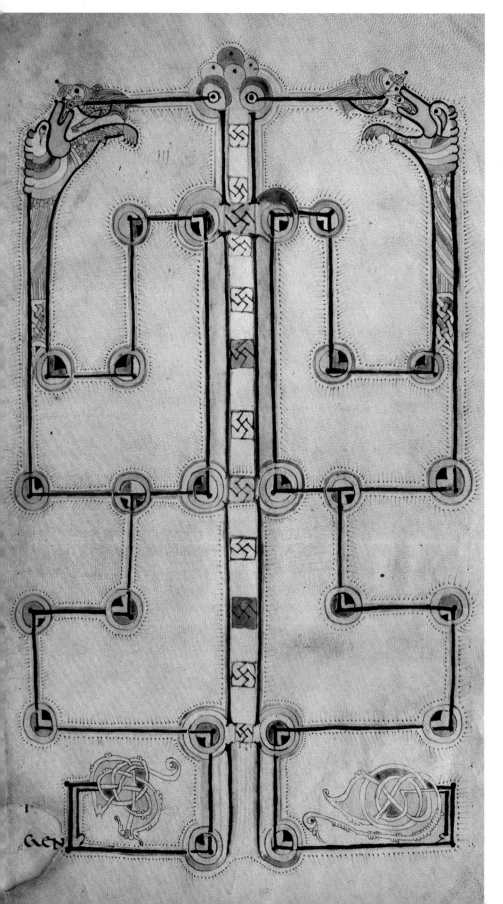

48 Many themes from pagan mythology were woven into early Irish and Anglo-Saxon art. This eighth-century manuscript shows two dragons on the world tree. The swastikas on the trunk represent the movement of the heavens around the cosmic axis. The twelve circles on each dragon most probably represent the twelve months of the year. And the confrontation of the solar eagles with the dragons, emissaries of the nocturnal world, suggest the alternation of night and day, the perennial battle of the forces of light and darkness. (Miniature from *Litterae paulinae*, Northumberland, 8th c. AD.)

49 Originally painted for the convent of Santa Chiara in Florence, this painting illustrates a religious text by St Bonadventure, the *Lignum vitae*, in which he traces the mysteries of the Origin, Passion and Glorification of Christ in twelve chapters. In this painting they are represented as the twelve branches of the Tree: the lowest four with medallions representing scenes relating to the Origin, the middle four to the Passion, and the top four to the Glorification of Christ. At the very top of the picture is Christ in Glory with the Madonna, and, below them, angels and saints. At the top of the Cross, between the prophets Daniel and Ezekiel, a pelican, traditional symbol for Christ's sacrifice. At the bottom of the picture, eight scenes from Genesis; above these, on the left, Moses and St Francis, and on the right, St John and St Clare. (Christ on the Tree of Life, painting by Pacino da Bonaguido, Italy, early 14th c.)

50, 51 The symbolism of the Scandinavian World Tree, Yggdrasil, is present in the regenerative curves and phantasmagoric interlacings of the carving on the left. On the right, a Viking memorial stone shows scenes relating to the cult of the high god Odin, who conquered death and gained 'the wisdom of the runes' after hanging for nine days and nights upon the World Tree. The warriors who fought in the name of Odin were known as 'beserkers': the god inspired them to wild frenzies of courage, releasing them from all inhibitions and the fear of death. The god also had the power to 'bind': to paralyse with terror and to lay the fetters of panic upon warriors in battle. This power to bind and loose is evident in the symbolism of knots and weaving, motifs often associated with Odin and the World Tree. It is especially present in Odin's talismanic symbol, the *valknut*, the three interlinked triangles to be seen here beside a ritual hanging, the traditional method of sacrifice to Odin. At the base of the stone is the ship of death, which denotes the journey to the other world. Above this, a scene representing the death of a warrior in battle. The eagle to be seen above the horse and the *valknut* represents the 'far-seeing' spirit form of Odin. For, in transcending the human condition, Odin, like the shaman, assumes an animal-spirit form to travel with absolute freedom through the spirit world. (50 Deer eating the World Tree, relief on the Stavkirke, Urnes, Norway: 51 Story of Odin, memorial stone from Läbro, Gotland.)

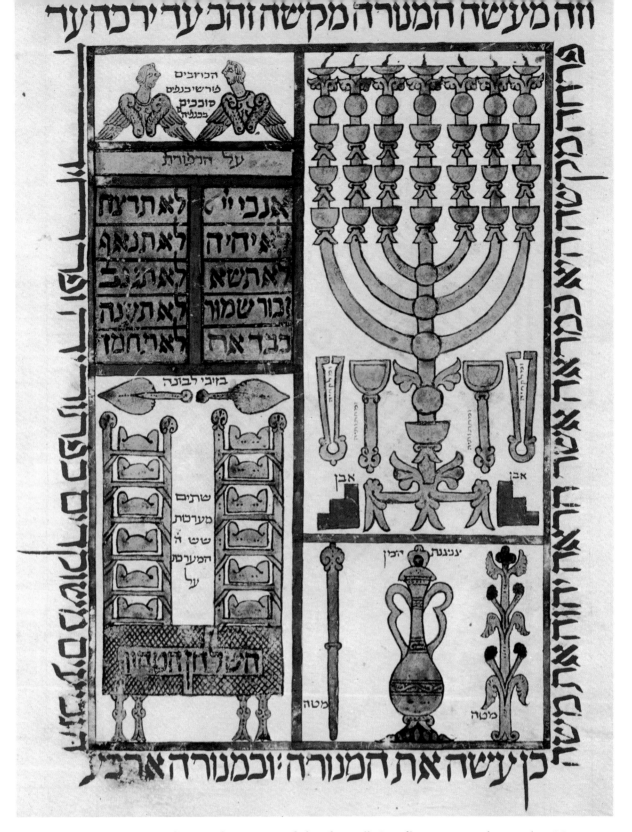

52 It was 'according to the pattern of the almond', Israel's most sacred tree, that Moses was instructed (Exodus 25:31–40) to make the cups, capitals and flowers of the original golden Menorah, whose origins are to be found in the Tree of Life' or Cosmic Tree of the ancient Near East (see p. 119). (Menorah with Greater and Lesser Masorah, Hebrew bible, Perpignan, 1299.)

53 'There shall come forth a rod out of the stem of Jesse, and a branch shall grow out of his roots and the Spirit of the Lord shall rest upon him.' (Isaiah 11:1–2.) In the tree which springs from the loins of Jesse are the figures of his descendants King David, The Virgin Mary and Christ. It was most likely the Jesse Tree, which first appeared in the twelfth century, that provided the model on which Joachim of Floris based his Tree of History (pl. 42). (Tree of Jesse, miniature from psalter of Henry of Blois, Winchester, 1140–60.)

54 Incorporating symbolic horse and solar wheel, this Celtic candelabrum suggests the chariot of the Sun, and shows the Pillar of the Universe at the centre of the turning world. Tree and horse are often symbolically related, as in the horse sacrifice and ritual ascent mentioned in the ancient Indian scriptures and found among the shamans of Siberia (who ascend to the sky world on the soul of a sacrificed horse). In Nordic myth it is to the World Tree (whose name is Yggdrasil, 'steed of Odin') that the great god Odin tethers his horse. (Horse with sun wheel, candelabrum, Celtic, Spain, 1st millennium BC.)

55, 56 Questioning the meaning of the visual image, the twentieth-century artist Marcel Duchamp removed this apparently meaningless Parisian bottlerack from its utilitarian context and exhibited it as a 'work of art'. In doing so, he drew attention to its dignity and power as a symbol. Placed next to this Buddhist Celestial Tree its latent symbolism is further brought out. (55 Buddha Tree with temple decoration, wood carving (now destroyed), China; 56 Bottlerack, readymade by Marcel Duchamp, galvanized iron, 1914.)

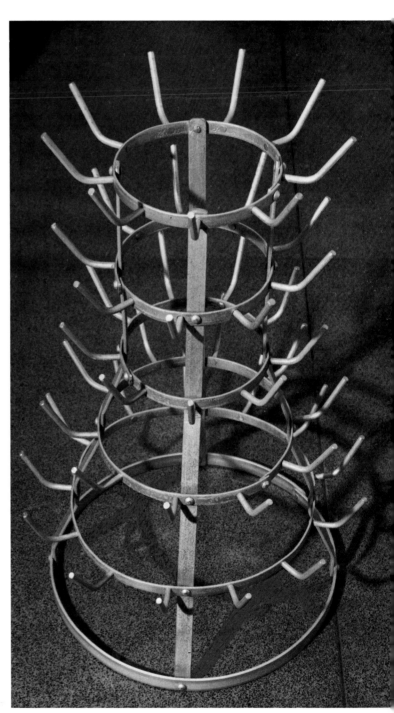

57 Many of the great pioneers of the modern movement in art found their own need to return to origins reflected in primitive and folk art. In this painting, the Russian artist Mikhail Larionov, returning to the primary images of Russian peasant art, recaptures the joys of a simple existence. The text on the painting reads: 'Happy Autumn – shining like gold – with ripe grapes – with wine that makes you drunk!' (Autumn, painting by Mikhail Larionov, 1911.)

58 Recapturing the world of childhood, reverie and imagination, Paul Klee puts together images and symbols which both singly and in combination have obsessed mankind for millennia: Ladder, Tree, House, Star, Bird and Cross. (Tree of Houses, watercolour by Paul Klee, 1918.)

Klee

1918   Der Häuserbau

59, 60 It is through the cosmic centre and along the Axis Mundi that the shaman travels when he makes his ecstatic ascents and descents to sky and underworld (p. 16). On the left, the Cosmic Tree growing from the 'soulship' or 'ship of the dead' which carries the Indonesian shaman to the other world. On the lower portion of the Siberian shaman's costume on the right, a scaly tree represents the shaman's descent through the centre (shown above) to the underworld. On the other side of this coat there is another tree representing the shaman's ascent to the sky world. (59 Tree of Life, detail of ceremonial cloth, Kroë, Sumatra; 60 Shaman's costume, Siberia, late 19th c.)

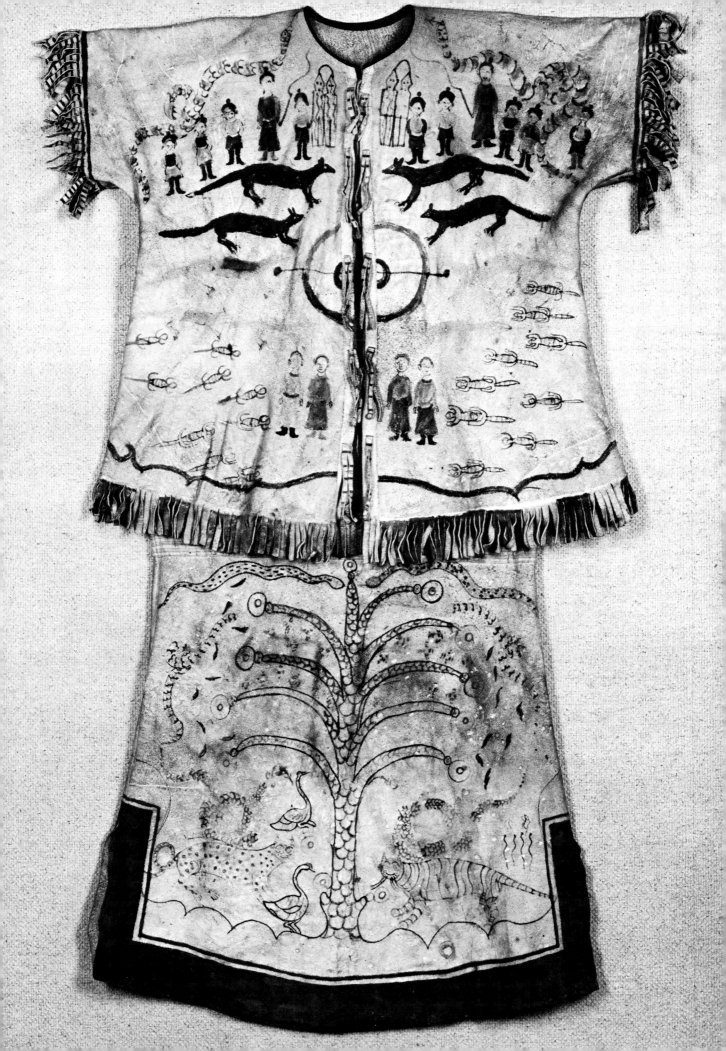

61, 62 The modern artist, like the 'primitive' shaman, extends the boundaries of being by ascending and descending into imaginary worlds. On the left, the Endless Column, Constantin Brancusi's version of the Axis Mundi (see pp. 126–27). Above, the image that appears in many of Joan Miró's paintings: he called it the 'ladder of escape'. (61 The Endless Column, cast iron sculpture by Constantin Brancusi, Public Park, Tirgu Jiu, Romania, 1937; 62 Dog Baying the Moon, painting by Joan Miró, 1926.)

63 Elements from Indian, Persian, Chinese and European art all combined to produce the 'flowering tree' motif that is the origin of chintz. Vast quantities of chintzes, painted cotton fabrics decorated with a central flowering tree, were shipped to Europe from India between the seventeenth and early nineteenth centuries. (Tree surrounded by animals, painted and dyed cotton, Palampore, India, 19th c.)

64 In Indian art and literature the two species of Indian fig, the asvattha and the banyan, are often confused. Only the banyan (pictured here) has long aerial roots which grow down from its branches and thicken into 'pillar-roots' or subsidiary trunks. It was most likely this species which provided the underlying image for the inverted Cosmic Tree mentioned in the *Rig Veda* and *Upanishads* – the Brahman rooted tree which exemplifies the manifestation of the sacred throughout the cosmos from a single transcendent root. (Temple in the trunk of a banyan tree, India.)

65 Through the work of Piet Mondrian the image of the Cosmic Tree played a
vital role in the radical transformations of modern art. Starting from his studies of a
real tree observed in nature, and working over a crucial period of approximately
five years, Mondrian produced numerous drawings and paintings in which the
cosmic aspect of the tree, represented by the weaving of its two vital axes, becomes
more and more apparent. Finally the image of the tree disappeared altogether,
leaving behind what Mondrian called 'the single primordial relation', the 'dynamic
equilibrium' or rhythm of vertical and horizontal, the cosmic axes of the universe.
This painting catches this process in mid-phase, when the observed image of the
real tree is gradually dissolving in the warp and weft of verticals and horizontals
(see pp. 124–5). (Horizontal Tree, painting by Piet Mondrian, 1911.)

Documentary illustrations
and commentaries

98

The Tree at the Centre

The 'wholly other' power that man has perennially experienced as the sacred radiates throughout the cosmos from its source at the centre (1, 2, 4), which as mid-point of the cosmos (3, 4, 5) ensures communication between the different cosmic levels of heaven, earth and underworld (7, 8).

Here, at the 'still point of the turning world', beneath the Bodhi Tree, the Buddha sat unmoved by the dazzling cosmic play of illusion (*maya*) that the god Kama-Mara, whose name means Love and Death, created before his eyes (6; see p. 21). At one with the centre of manifestation, his divine compassion radiates throughout the cosmos, drawing the hearts of all beings towards the centre and the source.

1 Worship of the Buddha-stupa and the Bodhi (Tree of Enlightenment). (Relief from Amaravati, 2nd c. AD, British Museum, London.)

2 Buddhist Stupa of Borobudur (Java, 8th c. AD.)

3 Maypole on Tynwald Hill, Isle of Man.

4 May Dance known as the 'Spider's Web', Ickley Green, Bedfordshire. In the spring or early summer the cosmos is recreated from the centre; the springtime rituals symbolically re-enact this event.

5 The Buddhist stupa is an image of the cosmos, through which the Axis Mundi passes. (Great Stupa of Sanchi, 1st c. AD.)

6 The Temptation of Buddha. (Relief from Borobudur, Java, 8th c. AD.)

7 The Tree as Cosmic Axis. (Rubbing from the altar of the Tamamushi temple, Nara, Japan, 7th c. AD.)

8 The Scandinavian World Tree, Yggdrasil. (Richard Folkard, *Plant Lore, Legends and Lyrics,* London, 1884.)

6

7

8

9

9 Shaman's drum from Lapland showing the three cosmic zones, sky, earth and underworld, joined by the Axis Mundi up which the shaman climbs. (Staatliches Museum für Völkerkunde, Munich.)

10 Shaman's drum from Lapland showing the world's centre, with the Axis Mundi in the form of a cross uniting the three worlds. (National Museum, Copenhagen.)

11 Navaho Indian sand painting showing the eight sacred plants growing from the centre. (Museum of Navaho Ceremonial Life, Santa Fe, N. Mex.)

12 Bamboo decoration of the Or-Danom Dayak of Borneo, showing the Tree of Life growing from a serpent in the underworld, and the universe represented as a house with the Axis Mundi passing through it, surmounted by a bird.

10

12

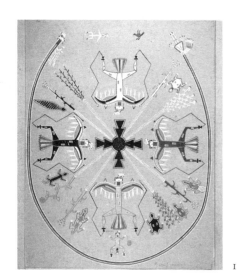

11

13

13 Cotton ceremonial cloth, showing the Tree of Life growing from the 'soul-ship' or 'ship of the dead' which carries the Indonesian shaman to the otherworld. (Kroë, Southern Sumatra.)

14 The Buddha, moved by compassion, shed a tear which changed into a lake full of lotuses. On one of them arose a goddess, represented here between the lotus and the crown, as the trunk of the celestial tree. (Relief on temple of Chandi Mendut, Java, 8th c. A D.)

15 The sacred asvattha tree (*Ficus religiosa*); in the left-hand corner, a diagrammatic representation of the sacred enclosure with a circular symbol of the centre, source of all creation and the point from which the cosmic tree grows. Horned beasts,

symbols of fertility and power, grow from the tree. (Seal, Mohenjodaro, *c.* 3000–1500 B C.)

16 In the earliest representations of Buddha's temptation, the Buddha is present but not represented. At one with the sacred which radiates throughout the cosmos, he is more truly represented by the Cosmic Tree. (Temptation of Buddha by Kama-Mara, Amaravati, 2nd c. B C.)

17 The sap of the sacred tree is the elixir of immortality, the ambrosia of the gods. An immortal hovers at the centre of the world, while a mythical hare pounds the elixir. (Kung O on the moon, bronze mirror-back, T'ang Dynasty, 7th–9th c. A D, Victoria and Albert Museum, London.)

14

16

15

17

18

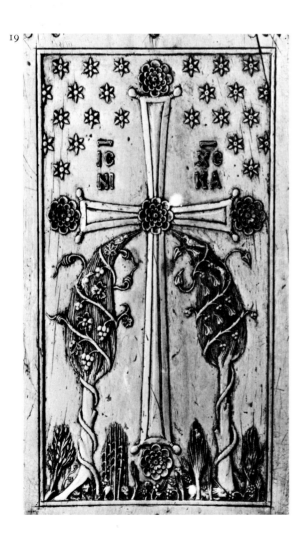

19

In Christianity the Cross embraces all the symbolism pertaining to the Tree at the Centre. Identified with the tree standing in 'the midst of the garden' in Paradise at the beginning of time, and with the tree at the centre of the Heavenly Jerusalem at the end of time, it unites the Alpha and Omega, the Beginning and the End, and represents the narrow path through the Centre, or the 'strait gate' between them. As the Tree of the Cross, 'It is the fulcrum of all things and the place where they are all at rest . . . the foundation of the round world, the centre of the cosmos' (Hippolytus of Rome; see pp. 20–21).

18 Coronation Mantle of the Holy Roman Emperors, made in the imperial workshops of King Roger II of Sicily at Palermo. (Kunsthistorisches Museum, Vienna.)

19 The Cross as the Tree at the Centre. Byzantine ivory. (Central panel of Harbaville Triptych, ivory, Byzantine, 10th–11th century, Louvre, Paris.)

20 The Tree of the Cross. Christ's monogram, the *chi-rho*, representing the axes of the cosmos, rises above the Cross as a symbol of the triumph of the Resurrection. (Detail of sarcophagus, 4th century AD. Museo Laterano, Rome.)

21 The royal sceptre and bishop's staff, often represented as a living branch, invest the holder with the centrality and power pertaining to the centre. (St Luke, St Chad Gospels, 8th century, Lichfield Cathedral.)

22 The Throne of St Mark in Venice is said to have come originally from Alexandria, where traditionally St Mark was bishop, and to have been given by the Emperor Heraclius to the Bishop of Grado in the 7th century. Beneath the Cross stands the Tree of Life with the Lamb of God upon a hill from which flow the four rivers of Paradise. (Throne of St Mark, St Mark's, Venice.)

20

21

22

Animal powers, monsters and gryphons guard the Tree of Life. Before one can attain the centre, eat the fruits of immortality, and drink the heavenly elixir of the gods, the sacred must be conquered and won.

23 The common iconographic motif of tree and confronted animals derives from the ancient Near East. Winged griffins guard the Tree of Life on this Assyrian seal. (Ward, *Cylinder Seals of Western Asia*, Washington, 1910.)

24 Here the same motif appears in a window from the abbey church of Santa Maria, consecrated in 1026. (Pomposa, Emilia, Italy.)

25 The animal hunt motif common to Christian and Islamic fabrics of the Byzantine period. (Textile, Constantinople, 8th c. A D, Vatican Museum.)

26 The Babylonian god Marduk fighting with the dragon Tiamat who embodies the dark disintegrating forces of chaos. Behind Marduk stand the World Pillar and the Tree of Life, on top of which sits a monkey. Beside the pillar is an antelope. (Ward, *Cylinder Seals of Western Asia*, Washington, 1910.)

Regeneration from the centre

The tree reveals the force of the sacred primarily by virtue of what it is in itself, through the power of its physical presence and through its seasonal transformations. Universally the earth is regarded as the 'mother of all things', and it is into the hidden and mysterious depths of this Great Earth Mother that the roots of the tree descend. Through these penetrating roots the tree participates in the regenerative life of the waters and the soil. From germination to death the tree remains bound to its mother the earth, the permanent source of its renewal. In the autumn, seed and leaf return to the earth out of which, from the mysterious rising of the sap in spring, they emerged. This sap, drawn from out of the depths, is the milk of the Great Goddess herself, the heavenly ambrosia, elixir of the gods, by means of which the dead attain immortality. Standing at the 'centre of all that surrounds it' the Tree of Life, like the Fountain of Life, is an image of the endless renewal of the cosmos from a single centre or source.

27 Many villages in India have their sacred tree. Here a woman waters the roots of the tree, those roots which draw up the regenerative juices in the Spring. In India, as elsewhere, trees are especially connected with all rites of renewal, with sexuality, fertility, conception, birth, initiation, death and rebirth.

28 The door of a temple in a sacred banyan tree, the tree whose trunk is made up entirely of roots (see pl. 64).

29 In dreams too, the tree appears as a symbol of renewal. In this spontaneously imagined painting the dreamer painted what he saw – a 'dark door' at the base of a tree. The door leads to the depths of the unconscious and signifies the need to renew a disturbed and troubled consciousness by making a return to the depths of psychic life. (The Dark Door, from Gerhard Adler, *Studies in Analytical Psychology*, London, 1967.)

30 The Tree of the Cross grows out of the body of the Virgin Mary. In Christianity the Virgin carries all the primary intuitions of the Great Earth Mother that are found in 'primitive' and archaic symbolism. Christ's sacrifice upon the Tree of Life perpetually renews the world. (The Dream of the Virgin, painting by Simone dei Crocifissi, 14th c., Pinacoteca Nazionale, Ferrara.)

31 Carved in the image of the Tree of Life, this font, at which the poet William Blake was christened, expresses the idea of the mystery of baptism as a rite of renewal in the 'waters of life' at the centre of the world. (Font by Grinling Gibbons, 1684, St James's, Piccadilly, London.)

31

30

32 The ancient Egyptians sought immortality. The celestial tree in this Egyptian tomb painting symbolizes perpetual renewal in the afterworld. (Tomb of Sennufer, Thebes, Deir-el Medineh.)

32

33

33 From the centre of an Egyptian celestial tree, planted in the 'waters of the depths', a goddess, epiphany of the Great Earth Mother, distributes the food and drink of immortality. (Detail from an Egyptian painting, 13th c. BC, I. Rosellini, *Monumenti dell' Egitto e della Nubia*, Pisa, 1832, pl. cxxiv.)

34 It was the 'dying god' or god of vegetation, Osiris, who gave the Egyptians hope concerning their own immortality. Trapped by his wicked brother Set, he was shut in a coffer and thrown into the sea. Where the coffer landed a tree grew round it. Later he was rescued by his beloved, the goddess Isis, who with the help of her sister Nepthys brought him back to life, an immortal life in the Egyptian afterworld. (Drawing from a relief, Dendera, Egypt, 1st c. BC.)

34

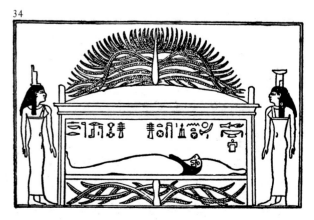

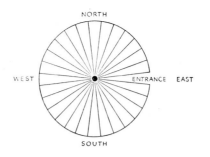

35

36

35, 36 It is at the centre that man renews his contact with the sacred, and this involves both suffering and joy. North American Indians have many rites of renewal which centre around a sacred tree or pole, symbol of the cosmic axis and of the perpetual regeneration of life. This drawing shows the sacred sun dance of the Sioux, when the bravest warriors pierce their breasts with leather thongs and dance around the centre dedicating their suffering and prayers to Wakan-Tanka, the Great Spirit who pervades the universe. The Oglala Sioux performed this dance in a sacred sun dance lodge. According to Black Elk, this lodge represents creation and the universe, each of the twenty-eight posts representing some object of creation as well as one of the phases of the lunar month, and the 'one tree at the centre is Wakan-Tanka, who is the centre of everything'. (Black Elk, *The Sacred Pipe*, London and New York, 1973.)

37 It is through joy rather than suffering that the Maypole dancers celebrate the rejuvenation of the cosmos in the Spring. Through their dance, and in the weaving of the bands, the dancers actively participate in the re-creation of the cosmos, the weaving of the world. (Maypole dance, Ickwell Green, Bedfordshire.)

38 In European folk festivals the spirit of vegetation was embodied in a variety of figures from Jack in Green to the King of the May. These figures would be dressed in leaves like this Congolese boy, who is dressed in foliage during his initiation rite to signify his personal rebirth into manhood.

37

38

The Tree of the Soul

The psychologist C. G. Jung understood the dream-image of the tree to be a symbol for the transpersonal Self, which, embracing the totality of conscious and unconscious processes, reflects the potential fullness of man's being. As such he distinguished it from the personal self or ego, centre of the field of consciousness, and warned of the disastrous consequences of their unconscious identification, which results in the mania of religious fanatics, tyrants, dictators and the insane.

39 In the Book of Daniel (ch. 4), King Nebuchadnezzar dreams of a great tree 'in the midst of the earth', around which all the 'beasts of the field' and 'birds of heaven' congregate. Then he sees 'a watcher and an holy one' come down from heaven crying: 'Hew down the tree, cut off his branches, shake off his leaves and scatter his fruit . . . and let his portion be with the grass in the earth. Let his heart be changed from a man's and let a beast's heart be given unto him.' Daniel interpreted this tree as representing the King himself who, in modern psychological terms, had identified his limited and personal self with the divine Selfhood which his kingship symbolized. It was this that finally brought about his madness, when his 'hairs were grown like eagle's feathers and his nails like bird's claws' and he regressed to the level of a beast of the field. (Nebuchadnezzar's Dream, from the Bible of Rodan, Bibliothèque Nationale, Paris, MS. lat. 6(3).)

39

40

41

44

Jung found that the unconscious works naturally, through the spontaneous imagery of dreams and fantasies, to help the individual actualize his own potential wholeness. This purposive process, which he called individuation, involves a sharpening of the moral opposites through an acknowledgment of the unconscious side of the personality. This tension of opposites within the individual is eventually followed by their reconciliation at a higher state of consciousness. Jung found confirmation for his discoveries concerning the nature and development of the psyche in the strange symbolic language of the alchemists, who sought to transform themselves by means of images and symbols which reflected the elemental transformation processes in nature. In this way the development of the Self gradually unfolds as a process of growth, which in both the hermetic language of alchemy and the symbolic language of dreams, is mirrored in the image of the tree.

40 The mysterious figure of Maria Prophetessa points to the mystery of transformation. (Michael Maier, *Symbolae aureae mensae*, Frankfurt, 1617.)

41 The process of transformation as a tree of the metals representing the astrological temperaments. (Hermetic Tree, from Basil Valentine, *Azoth*, 1659.)

42 The alchemical process represented as a tree with the seven stages on the stem from which grow the two branches of the body (*corpus*) and soul (*anima*), from whose union the alchemical symbol of the totality of the Self, the *Lapis* or Philosophers' Stone, is made. (Twelve alchemical operations, from Samuel Norton, *Mercurius redivivus*, 1630.)

43 Diagram of the human sensibility as a plant rooted in the 'dream life' by Carl Gustav Carus (1789–1869), an important precursor of the theory of the unconscious. (C. G. Carus, *Natur und Idee*, Leipzig, 1861.)

44 The transformation process is represented in this Indian miniature by the tree and by Radha and Krishna who symbolize the union of spirit and matter. (Radha and Krishna, miniature, Victoria and Albert Museum, London.)

45, 46 Both these images arose spontaneously from the unconscious, and both had a specific meaning in relation to the persons who painted them. Concerning the first (45), Jung stresses the dangers of an easy identification with the unconscious image of the Self, and the need for conscious Self-realization. 'A person whose roots are above as well as below is thus like a tree growing simultaneously downwards and upwards. The goal is neither height nor depth, but the centre.' Jung's caption for the second (46) reads: 'Union of opposites represented by two trees growing into one another and joined by a ring. The crocodiles in the water are the separated opposites, which are therefore dangerous.' (C. G. Jung, 'The Philosophical Tree', in *Alchemical Studies*, London and New York, 1967.)

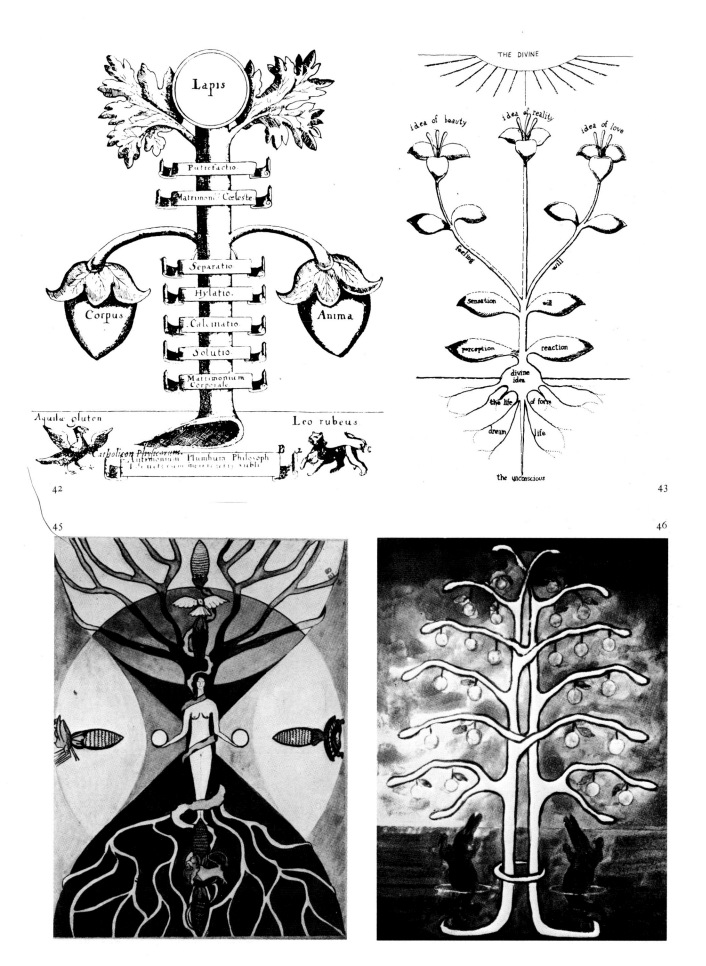

42

43

45

46

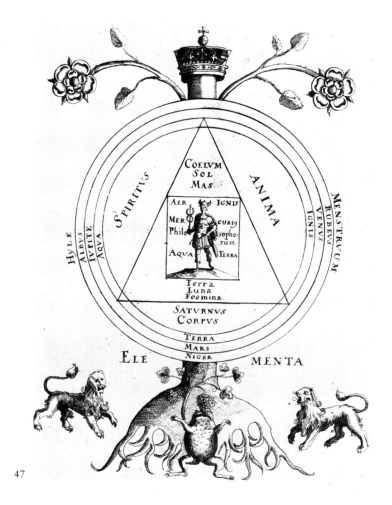

47

48

47, 48 In this alchemical tree the transformation process is represented as a two-, three- and fourfold union of opposites. On the circles; solid and fluid, white, black and red, Jupiter, Mars and Venus, water, earth and fire. Around the triangle; spirit, soul and body. Within the triangle; heaven, sun, male, and earth, moon and female. Within the square, the four elements, air, fire, water and earth. Surmounting the tree between its red and white roses is the crown, symbol of unity. In the centre of the square stands the spirit who presides over the whole process, Mercury or Hermes, god of healing, messenger of the gods and master of the Hermetic arts. He wears a winged helmet and carries his staff, known as the Caduceus (48), which is a potent image of transformation and progress through the union and strife of the opposites. (47 Hermetic transformation, from Samuel Norton, *Mercurius redivivus*, 1630; 48 Caduceus, woodcut, Swiss, 1615.)

Tree and Serpent

It was the power and wisdom of the serpent that awoke Adam and Eve from their dreaming innocence in the Garden. It awoke them to the true conditions of existence, to an awareness of the world, and to a mutual recognition of each other's 'otherness'. Looked at from another frame of reference one could say that their Kundalini, their serpent power or life force, was awakened. For it is not only in Genesis that one finds the serpent related to the tree. Associated universally with sexuality, fertility, and rebirth, the serpent embodies the regenerative powers of the waters that rise up through the tree from the depths of the earth. The movement of these waters, through the universe and through the tree, is governed by the endlessly repeated waxing and waning of the moon. The serpent too, through its movements and behaviour, its mysterious appearances and disappearances in and out of the earth, and in the periodical sloughing of its skin, embodies the cycles of the moon, the heavenly body that above all others governs the rhythms of existence.

49 Eve takes the fruit from the mouth of the serpent. (*Codex vigilanus*, San Lorenzo del Escorial, Spain.)

50 The so-called 'Seal of Temptation', which in fact represents the Sumerian goddess Gala Bau, epiphany of the Great Earth Mother, on the left of the tree. Behind her is the serpent, emblem of the powers she represents. On the left of the tree sits her son-lover, Dumuzi, the ever-dying, ever-resurrected god of vegetation, 'Son of the Abyss: Lord of the Tree of Life'. (Ward, *Cylinder Seals of Western Asia*, Washington, 1910.)

51 In the special form of Indian yoga known as Kundalini yoga, the human body is conceived as a microcosm, in which the spinal column is the Axis Mundi. The life force, closely allied with sexuality, is imagined as the serpent Kundalini, which sleeps at the base of the 'spinal tree'. The task of the yogi is to arouse this sleeping force, and get it to climb the spinal tree, piercing the various spiritual centres (chakras) on the way, until finally it is released from the Sahasrara Chakra, the Thousand-petalled Lotus at the top of the head. This difficult ascent follows a twofold path, representing the tension between the dynamic polarities of life. At the different planes of being, symbolized by the ascending chakras, the tension is resolved: the paths cross, and a breakthrough in consciousness is achieved. This motif of intertwining serpents is an archetypal model for spiritual and psychological development, also found in our Western spiritual tradition as the Caduceus, the staff of Hermes, healer of souls, messenger of the gods, and master of the Hermetic art of alchemy. (See 47, 48, opposite.)

49

50

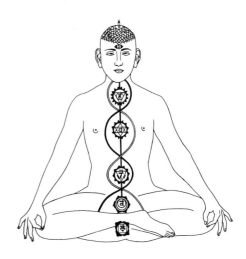

51

52

53

54

52 The serpent coils up the World Tree between its two fruits. On either side, symbols of the sun and moon, showing that it stands at the centre of the world, the place where 'the moon does not wane and the sun does not set'. (Detail of bowl, Elamite, late Sassanian, AD 226–641.)

53 Two vipers twine around a central axis in the manner of the Caduceus, on this steatite vase inscribed by King Gudea of Lagash to the god Ningizzida, 'Lord of the Tree of Truth.' (Vase, green steatite, Sumerian, *c.* 2400 BC, Louvre, Paris.)

54 On the side of this Irish Celtic cross, the hand of God, *Dextra Dei*, is shown above two serpents ascending and descending around an axis of three heads, probably heads of the saints who have gained mastery over the vital forces. (Cross of Muiredach, Monasterboice.)

55 After being decorated with serpent forms, these stone tablets called nagakals are placed for some six months in a pond to become imbued with the regenerative energies present in its muddy waters. After this they are set up, preferably beneath a sacred tree, as a votive gift by women desiring an offspring. (Votive stones, Sriringapatna, India.)

56 At the popular level the power to charm snakes by music reflects the ability to control the vital energies and forces active both in nature and in man. (Ascetic with snake, miniature, Deccan, late 18th c., Victoria and Albert Museum, London.)

57 As the embodiment of the watery lunar principle, the serpent is often represented as in conflict with solar animals, like the lion and the eagle. In this Egyptian painting the solar animal is a cat. (Tomb of Inkherka, Egypt, 16th–14th c. BC.)

55

56

57

The Tree of Ascent

As symbol of the centre, meeting-point of the three cosmic planes, the Cosmic Tree (like the Cosmic Mountain) has been perennially associated with rites, myths and symbols of ascent. For it is through the centre of the world and along the Axis Mundi that men and gods maintain communication with each other, ascending and descending to sky, earth and underworld.

58 The shamans of Siberia make their ascents and descents to the spirit worlds above and below in religious ecstasy and trance. Here, the shaman Tulayev stands before his tent (*yurt*), holding his drum. It is believed by many Siberian tribes that the frame of the shaman's drum is made from the wood of the great World Tree which stands on an island or a mountain at the centre of the world. This relationship between the Tree and the drum is extremely significant, for it is through his drumming that the shaman induces the religious ecstasy that enables him to enter the trance state and ascend through the centre to the spirit world. His spiritual vocation first manifests itself quite involuntarily, in the form of spontaneous dreams and visions, during which he is initiated by the spirits of the other world. This consists, in part, of being 'cut to pieces' and 'reduced to a skeleton', then mystically remade from the bones which represent the indestructible 'essence' of life. As a sign that he has undergone this process, the shaman here wears the skeletal structure of his rib cage appliquéd to his chest. This is sewn on with the white throat hairs of the reindeer, the sacred thread used for all ritual embroideries. Altogether the shaman's costume is extremely sacred, for as soon as he puts it on he is in contact with the spirits of the other world, because the costume which is decorated with their symbols is impregnated by their power. (Karagass shaman, Siberia, photographed by Petri, *c.* 1927.)

59 It was from the centre, along the Axis Mundi, that Christ, Buddha and Mohammed all made their ascensions. Here, Christ ascends to heaven up the Tree of the Cross. (Relief, bronze, San Zenone, Verona, 11th c.)

60 Design from a shaman's drum, showing the Axis Mundi ascending to the sky world. The circle around it at the top most likely represents the 'smoke-hole' of the celestial vault, which is imagined as a vast tent of stretched skin. The shaman is represented on the left holding a drum.

61 The thin line represents the shaman's path to the supreme god Bai Ulgen. It begins at the tent of the family for which the ritual takes place, and leads past the sacrificial horse, on whose soul the shaman rides on his ascent, to the shaman's specially constructed tent. This has a birch tree placed through its centre (61) with nine steps cut into it. Beyond this the path continues with representations of various events on the way. At the very top is Bai Ulgen surrounded by rays of light. (Drawing of a shaman's ascent to heaven, Altai region, Siberia.)

62 Drawing of a shaman's tent showing the ritual birch passing through the centre. (Tungus, Manchuria.)

63 Quite common among 'primitive' peoples is the belief that the Supreme Being dwelt on earth whilst he was still engaged in its creation; but that on completing it, he disappeared forever into the sky. For the Australian Arunta tribe, the Alchipa, the sacred pole they always carried with them was the pole up which their creator god Numbakula had climbed. It is recorded that once this pole got broken: upon which the whole clan ceased their desert wanderings and lay down to die. For the axis of their world was broken, and communication with the sacred world was lost. (Spencer and Gillen, *The Arunta*, London, 1927.)

64 The shaman's ascent of the World Tree represented on a ceremonial textile. (Soemba, Indonesia.)

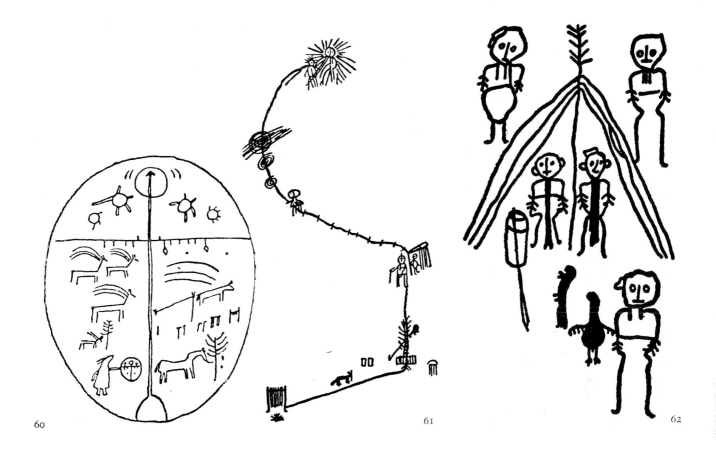

60   61   62

63

64

65

65, 66 The theme of ascent through the centre is powerfully evoked in Indonesian art by the winged-mountain-tree-door motif. It always appears on the most important object of the Javanese shadow theatre, the *gunungan* ('mountain') or *kekayon* ('tree'; see pl. 21). Above (65), it appears in Javanese sacred architecture, above and around the doorway, and to its right. Here it evokes the double theme of 'passing through' and 'ascent' to another world, another plane of being. (65 Gateway B of temple, Sendangdunur Badjanegara, Java; 66 *Gunungan*, leather, Java.)

66

The Tree of Light

Burning trees and bushes are well known to the history of religions, mythology and folklore, for the sacred often manifests itself as fire and light. The life-giving liquids, drawn up from the roots through the tree, are concentrated and transformed as they ascend. The sap of the tree becomes the precious 'oil of life' that burns in fruit and flower.

In Judaism, the Tree of Life is most often represented by the flowering almond tree, the tree which, in the Near East, heralds and hastens the spring, its radiant white blossoms appearing long before its leaves. It was to the pattern of the almond that Moses was instructed to make the cups, capitals and flowers of the sevenbranched candlestick, the Menorah (Exodus 25:31–40). In this and in the Sephirotic Tree of Jewish Kabbalists, the cosmic symbolism of the Divine Light and the cosmic symbolism of the Tree of Life are combined.

68

67 The Menorah derives both in form and symbolism from the model of the sacred tree in the ancient Near East. (Design from stone vase, Mesopotamian, before 3000 BC.)

68 The golden Menorah being carried off from the Temple during the sack of Jerusalem. (Arch of Titus, Rome, after AD 81.)

69 This picture, by a patient of Jung's, shows the Tree of Light as a dream-image which arose spontaneously out of the unconscious. Psychologically, it signifies the expansion and illumination of consciousness. (C. G. Jung, *Alchemical Studies*, London and New York, 1967.)

67

69

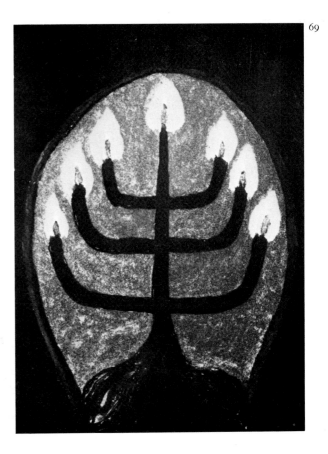

In the Kabbalah, it is down through the ten 'spheres' or Sephiroth, which represent the creative emanations of God's innermost being, that the Divine Light is refracted and reflected. These make up the Sephirotic Tree of Life, which unfolds the hidden structure of God, Man and the Universe, which in the En Sof, the Infinite, are inseparably one. The Divine Light which is reflected in the Sephiroth is like the light of the sun which is reflected in the heavenly spheres, and so each of the seven lowest spheres in the tree is associated with one of the heavenly bodies. In the diagram (70) each has its astrological sign according to the system used by Kircher: Tifereth–Beauty–Sun, in the centre, and beneath, Hod–Splendour–Venus, Netsah–Firmness–Mars, Yesod–Foundation–Mercury, Malkuth–Kingdom–Moon, and above, on the left, Din or Gevurah–Judgment–Saturn, and on the right, Hesed–Love–Jupiter. This astrological symbolism is also to be found in the Menorah, which is shown in a traditional Kabbalistic diagram (71) with the Hebrew letters for the ten Sephiroth on its stem and branches.

70 Sephirotic Tree. (Engraving from Athanasius Kircher, *Oedipus aegyptiacus*, 1652.)
71 The Sephiroth related to the Menorah. (Bibliothèque de l'Alliance Israélite Universelle.)
72 Jonah beneath the gourd. (From a Biblical MS., 14th c., British Museum, London.)

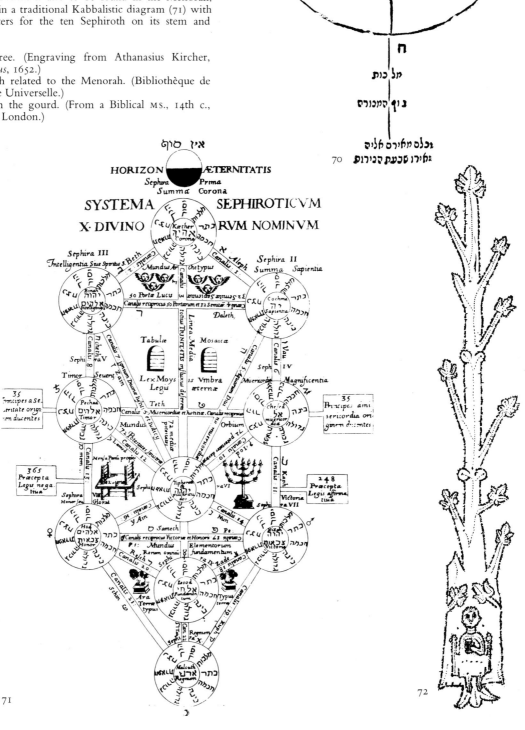

73

The Tree and the Cross

Since Judaeo-Christian times, before it spread to the Graeco-Roman world, Christianity has recognized a profound mystical link between the Cross of Christ and the Tree of Life. Uniting the Alpha and the Omega, past and future, beginning and end, the Tree of the Cross stands between the Tree of Life in Paradise (Genesis 2:9) and the Tree of Life in the world to come (Revelation 22:1–2.)

It is at once the Tree of Suffering, through which the tragic tensions and polarities of existence are revealed, like the tree of which Adam originally ate, *and* the Tree of Salvation, by means of which the perpetual crisis of existence, the estrangement, suffering and guilt caused by Adam's 'sin', are accepted and overcome.

74

75

76

73 Stele from a cemetery belonging to a Christian Gnostic sect, the Archontici. Shown are circular symbols of the centre, the tree, palm branches and the cross. The bird has been interpreted as the Phoenix, symbolizing Christ's resurrection. (Cemetery, Khirbet Kilkis, near Hebron, Israel, 4th c. AD.)

74 Stone cross from Ireland, showing, at the centre, Adam and Eve on either side of the Tree of Life. (North Cross, Castledermot, Kildare.)

75 Inscriptions from the Judaeo-Christian tomb at Bethpage, which relate to the millennarian beliefs of the early Christians. Left to right: the symbol of 1000, the Tree of Life (both linked to millennarian themes in the Old Testament) and Greek and Hebrew letters each with a complex symbolic meaning. (Detail of tomb of Nur, Bethpage, Israel.)

76 The Tree that brought about Man's Fall is also the source of his Redemption. (*The Mystery of the Fall and Redemption of Man*, by Giovanni da Modena, Bologna, 15th c.)

77–85 These woodcuts illustrate a popular medieval legend concerning the mysterious relationship between the Cross of Christ and the Tree of Life. It exists in many different versions; these versions, and the story's complex origins in ancient Mesopotamian mythology and in Jewish apocalyptic writings, have been studied by E. C. Quinn (*The Quest of Seth*, Chicago, 1962.)

Adam, 932 years old and dying, calls his son Seth to his side and tells him to go to Paradise to fetch the oil of mercy (77). As instructed, Seth retraces the path taken by his parents after the Fall, following their blackened footprints through a bleak and barren landscape. As he approaches Paradise, the landscape gradually changes, until the air is filled with music and the scent of grass and flowers. He wanders on, forgetful of his task, wholly absorbed in the beauty which surrounds him, when suddenly there flashes before him a vertical line of fire. It is the flaming sword of the Archangel Michael, who guards the gates of Paradise. Seth falls to his knees, unable to utter a word, but the angel knows his errand, and tells him that the time of Adam's pardon is not yet come. 'Four thousand years must pass,' he says, 'before the Redeemer opens the gates closed by Adam's disobedience.' But, as a token of future pardon, the wood from which mankind's redemption shall be won will grow from Adam's grave (78).

77

The angel then invites Seth to look into Paradise three times. The first time, he sees a marvellous fountain at the meeting-point of four rivers; behind it stands a withered and barkless tree. The second time, he sees a frightful serpent coiling round the trunk of this tree, which hangs above an abyss in which he sees his brother Cain struggling, enmeshed in the fibrous roots of the tree, which penetrate his body. Horrorstruck, Seth looks away. When he looks for the last time, he beholds a magnificent tree spreading wide and reaching up to heaven. In its topmost branches is a marvellous child, watching seven white doves circling above his head. The child sits in the lap of the most beautiful woman Seth has ever seen. The angel tells him that this child is the second Adam, the future Redeemer of the sins of all mankind. Finally he gives him three seeds from the fruit of this mighty tree, telling him that on his return in three days, Adam will die, and he is to place them on Adam's tongue (79).

When Seth returns, Adam hears the story and laughs for the first time since his banishment from Paradise. After his death three trees grow up from his body; a cypress, a pine and a cedar (80). In the course of time the branches of these trees touch, and their roots entwine to form one magnificent tree, the noblest of all in Lebanon (81).

78

The second part of the legend deals with an infinitely variable number of episodes relating this miraculous tree to the events of the Old Testament. Moses transplants it to Mount Tabor, and uses a branch from it to bring forth water from the rock in the wilderness and to divide the Red Sea so that the children of Israel can flee the armies of Pharaoh, and on it he hangs the brazen serpent so that all who behold it are delivered of the plague of snakes. This branch is also Aaron's branch. Later King David bewails his sins beneath it, and in one version transplants it to Jerusalem. King Solomon tries to convert it into the main pillar for his palace (82), but the tree-pillar changes its height at will. When he lowers the walls of his palace to accommodate it, it shoots up and pierces the roof. Exasperated, he casts it into a brook, where it is used as a crossing and is trodden underfoot (83). The Queen of Sheba, however, recognizing its virtue, refuses to set her foot upon it, preferring to wade through the stream (84). Finally Solomon buries it, later digging a pool on the same spot. This pool acquires miraculous properties, so that the sick and lame come to bathe in it and be made whole.

As the time for the Crucifixion draws near, the wooden beam floats mysteriously to the surface of the pool, where it is eventually found by the Roman centurions who use it to form the cross on which Christ is crucified. This cross is set up in the precise spot, the navel of the world, where Adam was created and died; this is Golgotha, the place of the skull. The blood of Christ falls on the skull of Adam at the base of the cross, thus baptizing the father of mankind and redeeming the sins of Adam's race (85). (*Illustrations from the Legendary History of the Cross . . . from a Dutch Book Published by Veldener, 1483*, ed. John Ashton, London, 1937.)

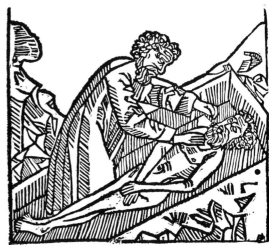

79

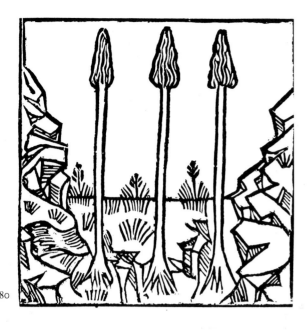

80

83

81

84

82

85

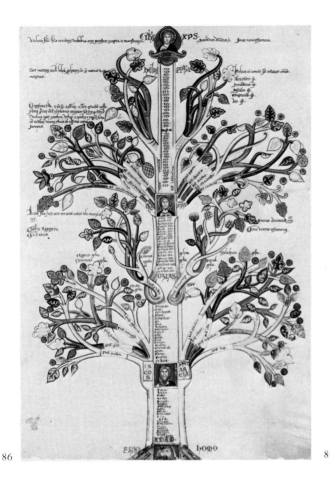

86

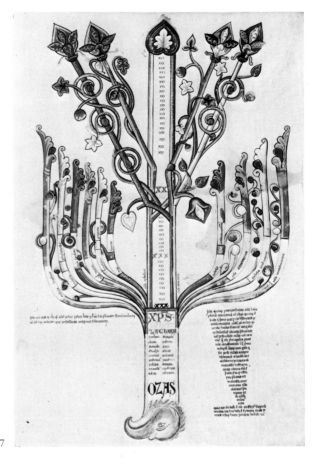

87

The Tree of History

Due to the influence of Joachim of Floris (1135–1202) the image of the tree played a vital role in moulding our modern conception of history (see p. 28 and pl. 42). What proved revolutionary in Joachim's Trinitarian vision of history was his conception of the overlapping of historical periods, periods of germination and fruition. For as each new shoot develops out of the one preceding it, so each period of history germinates the one to follow.

86, 87 The generations based on Matthew 1 in Joachim's trees of history go from Adam through Jacob and Hosea to Christ. In both these *figurae* there are forty-two generations leading on from Christ, each one represented by the Roman numerals XXX (i.e. 30 years); 42 × 30 = 1,260, and AD 1260 was the year which the Joachites set as the beginning of the germination period for the third stage of history, the age of the Holy Spirit. (Joachim of Floris, *Liber figurarum*, 13th–14th c., Seminario Vescovile, Reggio Emilia.)

Modern images of the Tree

88

polarities of life: the perpetual interpenetration of male and female, active and passive, spirit and matter, universal and unique. Having achieved their distillation during this critical period Mondrian spent the rest of his working life painting celebrations of the 'mystical marriage', *hieros gamos*, or, as he called it, 'dynamic equilibrium', of this primordial pair.

88 Tree II, drawing by Piet Mondrian, 1912. (Haags Gemeentemuseum, The Hague.)
89 Tree, painting by Piet·Mondrian, *c.* 1912. (Museum of Art, Carnegie Institute, Washington, D.C.)
90 Composition, painting by Piet Mondrian, 1913. (Rijksmuseum Kröller-Müller, Otterloo.)
91 Composition, painting by Piet Mondrian, 1921. (Öffentliche Kunstsammlung, Basle.)

89

90

'To find nature herself, all her likenesses have to be shattered; and the further in, the nearer the actual thing.' This sentence from the writings of the medieval German mystic Meister Eckhart aptly characterizes the modern movement in art. For all the most important artists of this century, in one way or another, have effected a 'return to origins', each re-experiencing for himself those primary images and forms in which man's spiritual and imaginary universe is grounded.

The painter Piet Mondrian rediscovered the primordial significance of the vertical and horizontal, a significance which is known to traditional man through the cosmic symbolism of weaving, where the union of warp and weft symbolizes the union of all the opposites (heaven and earth, etc.) upon which the fabric of existence is woven.

The appearance of the image of the tree in Mondrian's work marks a crucial turning-point in its development. Starting from his studies of a real tree, and working over a period of approximately five years (1908–13), Mondrian produced a series of studies in which its cosmic aspect becomes more and more evident. Through a long process of refinement and distillation the outer image of the tree gradually dissolves, finally disappearing altogether. What remains are its vertical and horizontal axes, the warp and weft out of which existence is woven and sustained. For Mondrian these symbolized all the dynamic

91

92

93

94

Another artist who made a significant as well as a profoundly personal 'return to origins' is the Romanian sculptor Constantin Brancusi (1876–1957) (92). Brancusi's life has all the makings of a myth. Born and brought up in a remote peasant community in the Carpathian mountains, where from the age of seven until nine he was a shepherd, he went on, by what he himself described as 'a succession of miracles' to become one of the leading artists of the Parisian avant-garde. Here, ironically enough, it was those very things which his training in the Western 'classical' tradition of sculpture had taught him to forget, that were to make him the father of modern sculpture.

98

The turning-point in his development came with the discovery of traditional African woodcarving by the small group of artists and poets to which he belonged. The strong symbolic form of these 'primitive' images led him back to his own native tradition, both to the boldly carved forms of peasant architecture (93, 94) and to the poetic images from Romanian folklore that had aroused his imagination in childhood.

One of these, which was to obsess him for practically the rest of his working life, is the famous 'Bird' or 'Maiastra' series. In this he explored the extremely archaic and universal theme of the 'soul-bird' (95–97), a theme which he knew from Romanian folk tales in which the 'soul-bird', Pasarea Maiastra, meaning 'miraculous bird', helps the hero in all his trials and combats. Some of these tales tell how the Maiastra succeeds in stealing the three golden apples which a miraculous apple tree produces each year, others how only a Prince can wound or capture the bird, and how once this is done she reveals herself as the Beloved for whom the Prince has been endlessly searching. At the beginning of this series Brancusi drew attention to the Maiastra's femininity by emphasizing the polished smoothness and rotundity of her breast, then gradually as the series progressed this mystery merged with another, the mystery of verticality and flight. 'I have searched during a whole life only for the essence of flight . . . flight – what happiness!' Brancusi said, to which Mircea Eliade has significantly added: 'He did not need to read books to discover that flight is the equivalent of happiness since it symbolizes ascent and transcendence of the human condition. Flight proclaims that heaviness is abolished, that an ontological change has taken place in the human being.'

The miraculous bird is associated with another of Brancusi's themes, the Endless Column (pl. 61). For this too, he returns to an image of his childhood, for the Column of the Sky is a common Romanian folk motif, which, though soon Christianized and referred to in Romanian Christmas carols, very probably reflects the characteristic beliefs of the megalithic culture of the third to fourth millennium B C. For it is, of course, the Axis Mundi, which passing through the centre of the world ensures communication between the three cosmic planes (heaven, earth and underworld).

95   96

97

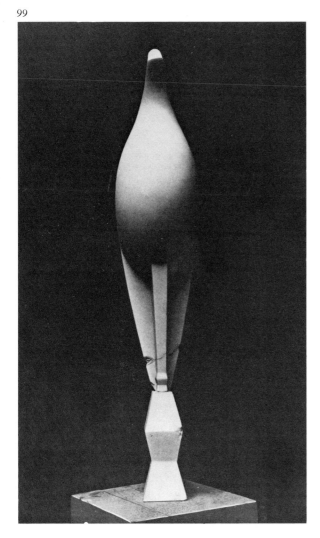

99

As Eliade has pointed out, Brancusi has made this symbolism evident by means of the indefinitely repeated rhomboidal forms, which relate it to the tree or pillar with notches cut into it, thus emphasizing the symbolism of climbing and ascent, for, as he says, 'in imagination one would like to climb up this "celestial tree".' And he goes on to say that Brancusi 'calls his column "endless" not only because such a column could never be completed but mainly because it launches itself into a space which can have no limits because it is founded on absolute liberty. It is the same space in which the "Birds" fly . . . But he has succeeded in revealing to his contemporaries that it is about ecstatic ascent without any mystical character – it is enough to allow oneself to be carried away by the power of the work to recover the grace of an existence free of any conditioning system.'

92 Brancusi sitting in an archway carved by himself in his Paris studio, 1946.

93 Wooden pillars from a peasant house at Ceauru, the region where Brancusi was born. (Musée du Village, Bucharest.)

94 Pillar found in the courtyard of a peasant house at Draghiceni, Oltenia.

95 Funerary pillar from the cemetery of Loman, region of Hundedoara, Transylvania. The bird is a symbol for the soul.

96 Wooden swans erected on poles above a platform on which a reindeer had been sacrificed. (Reindeer Tungus, Manchuria.)

97 This miniature painting, from the same manuscript as pl. 32, illustrates the Persian mystic's quest for the beloved. She appears to him time and time again in the guise of the 'soul-bird' before finally revealing her identity.

98 Brancusi's studio, 1928, showing oak versions of his Endless Column, also the Fish and on the right his Socrates.

99 In this version Brancusi places the bird on a segment of the Endless Column. (Bird, 1915, marble, Atelier Brancusi, Musée National d'Art Moderne, Paris.)

100 In his famous public lecture of 1924, published under the title *On Modern Art*, Paul Klee used the image of the tree to show how the artist is a medium or channel for the transformative processes of nature. 'From the roots the sap rises up into the artist, flows through him and his eyes. He is the trunk of the tree. Seized and moved by the force of the current, he directs his vision into his work. Visible on all sides, the crown of the tree unfolds in space and time. And so with the work.' In this drawing Klee places the upright of the K in his signature through the centre of the trunk of the tree, thus symbolically uniting his own creative powers with those of nature herself. (The Fir Tree, drawing by Paul Klee, 1940, Collection Felix Klee, Berne.)

Sources of quotations

William Blake, *A Vision of the Last Judgment,* in *Complete Writings,* ed. Geoffrey Keynes, London, 1966.

Black Elk, *Black Elk Speaks,* Lincoln, Nebr., 1961.

Henry Corbin, 'Mundus Imaginalis or the Imaginary and the Imaginal', *Spring,* New York, 1972.

Henry Corbin, *Creative Imagination in the Sufism of Ibn 'Arabi,* London and Princeton, 1969.

Gaston Bachelard, *On Poetic Imagination and Reverie,* Indianapolis and New York, 1971.

Mircea Eliade, *Cosmos and History: the Myth of the Eternal Return,* New York, 1954.

Mircea Eliade, *Images and Symbols,* London and New York, 1961.

Voluspä: quoted by Mircea Eliade, *From Primitives to Zen: a Thematic Source Book on the History of Religions,* London and New York, 1967.

Yakut myth: quoted by Uno Holmberg, *Mythology of All Races, IV: Finno-Ugric, Siberian,* New York, 1964.

J. G. Frazer, *The Golden Bough,* abridged edition, London and New York, 1957.

Baldwin Spencer and F. J. Gillen, *The Arunta,* London, 1927, vol. I.

Mircea Eliade, *Shamanism: Archaic Techniques of Ecstasy,* London and New York, 1970.

Gershom Scholem, *Major Trends in Jewish Mysticism,* New York, 1954, and London, 1955.

Gershom Scholem, *On the Kabbalah and its Symbolism,* New York, 1969.

Black Elk, *The Sacred Pipe,* Lincoln, Nebr., and London, 1973.

Hippolytus of Rome: quoted by Hugo Rahner, 'Christian and Pagan Mysteries', in *Papers from the Eranos Yearbooks, 2: The Mysteries,* Princeton, 1965.

M. Beckwith, *Hawaiian Mythology,* New Haven, 1940.

Paul Tillich, *Systematic Theology,* London and Chicago, 1957.

Carl Gustav Jung, 'The Philosophical Tree', in *Alchemical Studies,* London and New York, 1967.

Rainer Maria Rilke, poem written in August 1914, in *Poems 1906–1926,* London 1959 (a different translation).

Abu Bayazid: quoted by A. J. Arberry, *Sufism: An Account of the Mystics of Islam,* London, 1950.

Hafiz: quoted by George Lechler, 'The Tree of Life in Indo-European and Islamic Cultures', *Ars Islamica,* vol. VI, 1937.

Marjorie Reeves and Beatrice Hirsch-Reich, *The Figurae of Joachim of Fiore,* Oxford, 1972.

Wassily Kandinsky, 'Reminiscences', in *Modern Artists on Art,* ed. Robert L. Herbert, New Jersey, 1964.

Paul Klee, *Notebooks, II: The Nature of Nature,* London and New York, 1973.

Paul Klee, *On Modern Art,* London, 1947.

Paul Carus, *Natur und Idee,* Leipzig, 1861.

Samuel Taylor Coleridge: quoted in M. H. Abrams, *The Mirror and the Lamp: Romantic Theory and Critical Tradition,* London, 1973, ch. 7, 8.

General sources and recommended further reading

Mircea Eliade, *Patterns in Comparative Religion,* London and New York, 1958, ch. 8.

E. O. James, *The Tree of Life: An Archaeological Study,* Leiden, 1966.

E. A. S. Butterworth, *The Tree at the Navel of the World,* Berlin, 1970.

F. D. K. Bosch, *The Golden Germ,* The Hague, 1960.

L. Yarden, *The Tree of Light, a Study of the Menorah,* London, 1971.

Shakti M. Gupta, *Plant Myths and Traditions in India,* Leiden, 1971.

Mircea Eliade, *Yoga, Immortality and Freedom.* New York, 1958.

Ionel Jianou, *Brancusi,* Paris, 1963.

Petru Comarnesco, Mircea Eliade and Ionel Jianou, *Témoignages sur Brancusi,* Paris, 1967.

Carl Gustav Jung, *Psychology and Alchemy,* London, 1953.